INCREDIBLE EDIBLE

Bible Story Fun

for Preschoolers

by

Jane C. Jarrell

and

Deborah L. Saathoff

Group

Loveland, Colorado

Incredible Edible Bible Story Fun for Preschoolers

Copyright © 1999 Jane C. Jarrell and Deborah L. Saathoff

Credits

Editors: Lori Haynes Niles and Dennis R. McLaughlin
Creative Development Editor: Dave Thornton
Chief Creative Officer: Joani Schultz
Copy Editor: Shirley Michaels
Art Director: Kari K. Monson
Cover Art Director/Designer: Jeff A. Storm
Computer Graphic Artist: Desktop Miracles
Illustrator: Mena Dolobowsky
Production Manager: Peggy Naylor
Cover Photographer: Index Stock Imagery

Library of Congress Cataloging-in-Publication Data

Jarrell, Jane Cabaniss, 1961–
    Incredible edible Bible story fun for preschoolers / by Jane C.
Jarrell and Deborah L. Saathoff.
      p.   cm.
   ISBN 0-7644-2108-5
   1. Christian education of preschool children. 2. Christian
education--Activity programs. 3. Cookery. I. Saathoff, Deborah
L., 1961–   . II. Title.
   BV1475.8.J37   1999
   268'.432--dc21
                                     98-42660
                                       CIP

10 9 8 7 6 5 4 3 2   08 07 06 05 04 03 02

Printed in the United States of America.

Visit our Web site: www.grouppublishing.com

Table of Contents

Introduction

Your preschoolers love to eat. And they love the satisfaction of doing something "all by themselves!" What a winning combination to help them remember Bible stories!

These Bible stories are some of kids' favorites, and they'll remember the stories even better when they make tasty treats to eat and share. The ingredients are simple, easy to obtain, and kid-approved. Plus, each recipe comes with a "Spice Up the Recipe!" option. This option offers additonal ingredients for more sophisticated flavors that will tantalize even dubious parents. The recipe cards can be photocopied so you can send them home and let families review the lessons together. Or you can make a lasting record of each child's Bible literacy by creating a card file of recipes for each one. Just photocopy the cards on card stock, have the children each draw a picture of the story on the back, and file the cards away.

You can use these recipes with your existing program or build an entire lesson by using the suggestions from "A Morsel More." Either way, your kids will be delighted with these *Incredible Edible* lessons about God's love.

A few simple tips will help your cooperative cooking efforts be most successful:

Handy Tips for Teachers

As you prepare for the activities in this book, keep the following guidelines in mind:

Cleanliness and Conservation

- Always make sure kids wash their hands before handling food items.
- Use a clean, damp cloth to thoroughly wipe all surfaces you'll be using. Keep a damp cloth handy throughout the activity, too!
- Involve all kids in the cleanup, and make sure you leave your area in good shape for the next group.
- Don't allow kids to waste food. If there's extra after your project is finished, be sure it gets used, or find someone to give it to.

Supplies

You may want to keep on hand these frequently used items:

- resealable plastic bags (quart-size freezer bags work best)
- napkins
- paper cups
- drinking straws
- washcloths
- paper plates
- plastic knives and spoons
- measuring cups and spoons

Old Testament

Animal Creations
We can thank God for the amazing animals he created.

Animal Creations

Terrific Tools:

measuring cups

paper plates or squares of wax paper (1 per child)

1 gallon-size resealable plastic bag

Fun Foods:

2 cups nonfat powdered milk

2 cups peanut butter

1 cup honey

Combine all ingredients in the resealable plastic bag. Seal the bag, and squeeze until the mixture forms soft, pliable dough. You may need to add more honey or powdered milk to get the desired consistency. Once the dough is prepared, divide it into individual portions.

(From Group Publishing, Inc.'s *Incredible Edible Bible Story Fun for Preschoolers;* copyright © 1999 Jane C. Jarrell and Deborah L. Saathoff.)

The Bible Story
God Creates Animals (Genesis 1)

Set out all premeasured ingredients along with the resealable plastic bag. Ask:
● How many different kinds of animals do you think there are?
● How did all the animals get here?

Say: When God first made this world, he filled it with beautiful trees and flowers. God made blue skies and warm sun for the day. God made a moon and billions of stars for the dark night. God made mountains and islands, oceans and jungles, deserts and forests. But God's new world still seemed empty. Ask:
● What do you think was missing?

Say: Let's make some dough so you can show us what you think was missing.

Have one child pour the powdered milk into the plastic bag, let another child add the peanut butter, and a third child add the honey. Say: **God worked** (start to squeeze the dough) **and worked** (pass the dough to a child) **and worked.** Pass the dough to a second child, and a third, and so on, until every child has had a chance to work the dough. Test the modeling dough. Make it stiffer by adding more powdered milk or softer by adding honey. Give each child a portion of the modeling dough and a plate or square of wax paper to set it on.

First, God filled the water and oceans. Use your modeling dough to show me what kind of animal you think God put into the sea. Let the kids share their creations. Sing this song to the tune of "If You're Happy and You Know It," substituting the names of the specific sea animals your kids mention:

Oh, God put the fish in the sea.
Oh, God put the whales in the sea.
Yes, God made them all,
The creatures great and small.
Oh, God put the fish in the sea.

Continue: **Next, God made all kinds of animals to fill the sky. Use your modeling dough to show me an animal God put in the sky.** After the children have shared their sky animals, sing the same song again, substituting kinds of sky animals your kids mention.

Oh, God put the owls in the sky.
Oh, God put the parrots in the sky.
Yes, God made them all,
The creatures great and small,
Yes, God put the birds in the sky.

Say: **After God made fish and birds, he made all different kinds of animals to live on land. Use your modeling dough to show me some land animals.** After the children have shared their land animals, sing the song, using the names of land animals they have formed.

Oh, God put the puppies on the land.
Oh, God put the elephants on the land.
Yes God made them all,
The creatures great and small.
Oh, God put the horses on the land.

Ask:
● **Do you think God made more than ten different animals?**
● **Did he make more than one hundred different animals?**

Say: **One scientist thinks God made over *five million* different kinds of animals. It would take over three months of counting to count all of those animals *if* you never stopped to sleep or eat. God thought up every single animal! God filled the world with amazing land animals, beautiful birds, and fantastic fish. Let's thank God for them.**

Pray: **Dear God, thank you for the animals you made that fill our world with wonder. Amen.**

Tell children to eat the animals up! As the kids munch, ask them to explain what animals are their favorites and why.

A Morsel More

🖐 Use a piece of light blue paper as a base for sky, and place a piece of brown below it for land and a piece of dark blue below the brown for sea. Let children place a variety of animal stickers in their proper habitats.

🖐 Get moving! Have the children move like different animals. Show them how to walk like a penguin or a crab, waddle like a duck, and slither like a snake.

🖐 Play Animal charades. Have a child act like or make the sound of an animal. Have the others guess which animal it is.

Spice Up the Recipe!

● Make your animals into masterpieces with currants for eyes, miniature chocolate chip morsels for noses, licorice for scarves, and cherry halves for hats.

● Give your animals stripes! Put icing in a small resealable bag. Cut a tiny corner off the bag, and let the children squirt the icing in vertical stripes all around the modeling dough animal.

fruit People
We can thank God for creating people.

---

fruit People

Terrific Tools:

paper plates (1 per child)

plastic knives

forks

paper towels

Fun Foods:

lettuce leaves, washed and patted dry (1 per child)

canned pear halves (1 per child)

canned peach halves (1 per child)

raisins (8 per child)

maraschino cherry halves (1 per child)

canned mandarin orange segments (4 per child)

Before class, use the plastic knife to make small slits on the peach half where the eyes, nose, and mouth would be. Scoop out a small place on the pear half near the top, in the center. This will be the place for the cherry heart.

Place a lettuce leaf on a paper plate. Place the pear half as the body and the peach half as the head, flat side down, on the lettuce leaf. Insert raisins in the slits in the peach half to form eyes, nose, and mouth. Place the cherry half in the indentation in the pear half. Arrange mandarin orange segments as arms and legs.

(From Group Publishing, Inc.'s *Incredible Edible Bible Story Fun for Preschoolers*; copyright © 1999 Jane C. Jarrell and Deborah L. Saathoff.)

The Bible Story
God Creates People (Genesis 2)

Say: After God created animals, he was still lonely. So he decided to make something extra special. He decided this creature would be a lot like him. Let's start making a model of his most special creation. If you figure out what it is, keep it a secret until the very end.

Give each child a lettuce leaf and a paper plate. Say: **First, let's make a bed for our special creation. Put the soft green lettuce on the paper plate.**

God made a head. Give each child a peach half. Place it, flat side down, near the top of the plate. **God made a body.** Give each child a pear half. Position it, flat side down, below the peach. Ask:

● **What creatures have a head and a body?**

Then God gave this new creature eyes that would see beauty. Give each child two raisins. Show the children how to place the raisins in the slits for the eyes. **Then God gave this new creature a nose that would smell flowers and food.** Give children each a raisin, and show them where to place the nose. Ask:

● **What creatures have eyes and noses?**

Say: **But then God gave this new creature a mouth that would sing his praises and would talk with him.** Ask:

● **What is the only creature that has a mouth to sing praises and talk with God?**

 page 10 • OLD TESTAMENT

Give each child four or five raisins to press into the peach along the line to form a mouth.

That creation was a human being! God gave this new person arms and hands that would do God's will, serve other people, and care for the beautiful new world God had made. God also gave this new person legs and feet to walk where God led and to dance with joy at all God had done. Give each child four mandarin orange segments to place on the pear as arms and legs.

Say: **Look at your body. You have eyes, a nose, a mouth, arms, and legs, just as your fruit person does. But what really makes this creature different from all the others is a part of you that you can't see. God gave this wonderful creation a special place that can be filled only by God's love.** Give each child a maraschino cherry half to place in the cavity in the pear.

When God made the day and night, he said they were good. When God made the land and water, he said they were good. When God made the plants, he said they were good. When God made the animals, he said they were good. But when God made the first human being, he said he was "very good." Because, you see, God made us so he could love us. And God wants us to love him, too. Ask:

● **What are some ways you can show God you love him?**

Encourage the children to use their wonderful mouths to talk to God.

Pray: **Dear God, thank you for making me. Thank you for loving me. Help me to show you my love for you. Amen.**

Enjoy your Fruit People!

A Morsel More

✋ Make outlines of the children's bodies. Ask each child to lie down on butcher or bulletin board paper. Use a dark crayon or marker to outline the shape of the child's body. Let the children use crayons or markers to fill in details such as hair, eyes, nose, mouth, clothes, and shoes so the drawings look like them.

✋ Examine thumb prints. Use water-based ink pads to make thumb prints. Examine them using magnifying glasses. Talk about the fact that no two people on earth have exactly the same swirls and designs on their thumbs.

Spice Up the Recipe!

● Use other foods to add more details to your people. Use half of a pineapple slice to make a necklace or chopped nuts to make a polka-dot shirt. Place licorice strings on the head for hair. Use dried bananas broken in half for a different kind of eyes. Cut a cored apple slice in half to make a great big smile. Let kids use their imaginations to create unique Fruit People.

Banana Boats and Animal Crackers
God will help us do the right thing.

Banana Boats and Animal Crackers

Terrific Tools:

snack-size resealable plastic bags (1 per child)

1 airtight container or 1 large resealable bag

plates (1 per child)

1 plastic knife

scissors

1 plastic glass

1 spoon

Fun Foods:

large bananas (1 per child)

strawberry cream cheese (1 tablespoon per child)

lemon-lime soda (1 can poured into a glass)

animal crackers (eight per child)

Before class, peel the bananas, and use a plastic knife to cut a lengthwise wedge out of the inner curve of each banana. Dip each banana in lemon-lime soda, and place it back in the peel. Store the bananas in an airtight container.

Place about one tablespoon of strawberry cream cheese near one corner of each resealable bag, and close it. Snip about one-half inch off the corner of the bag, near the cream cheese, so the kids can squeeze it out. Place four animal crackers, flat side up, on a plate. Squeeze a little strawberry cream cheese on each one. Place four other animal crackers on top of the corresponding animals, and press the pairs together. Place the animal cracker sandwiches in the banana boats.

(From Group Publishing, Inc.'s *Incredible Edible Bible Story Fun for Preschoolers*;
copyright © 1999 Jane C. Jarrell and Deborah L. Saathoff.)

The Bible Story
Noah and the Ark (Genesis 6–8)

Ask:

● Have you ever been with people who were doing something you knew wasn't the right thing to do? How did you feel? What did you do?

Say: Many years after God created people, people forgot about God. They didn't pray anymore. They didn't think about pleasing God. They said and did mean things to each other. God was very sorry he had made them, so God decided to put an end to all people. But the Bible tells us that, out of all the people in the world, one man pleased God. He had not forgotten about God. He prayed to God. He lived his life trying to do things that made God happy. He spoke kind words and treated other people fairly and with kindness, even though no one else around him did.

That man's name was Noah. God decided he would start all over again, so he told Noah to build a big boat called an ark. God told Noah what should be used to make it. Hand each child a banana. God told Noah exactly how it should be built. Have the children remove the peels. See how there's a space inside this special banana boat? What do you think God told Noah to put into the boat?

God told Noah to find two of every kind of animal, a boy and a girl of each

one. Let each child look for matching pairs of animal crackers, and take four pairs. Show them how to place one of each pair, flat side up, on the paper plate. Show them how to squeeze a little strawberry cream cheese on each cracker and then place the matching animal crackers on the cream cheese to form sandwiches. (One cracker will have the flat side facing out if they are matched them head to head.)

Noah obeyed God. He gathered the animals and placed them in the ark. Have the children place their animal sandwiches in the banana arks.

When Noah and his family and all the animals were in the ark, God shut the door. Soon rain began to fall. It rained so long the entire earth was covered with water, but Noah, his family, and all the animals were safe inside the ark.

After a long time, the rain stopped. The waters slowly went down until all the animals and people inside the ark could go out on dry land.

Noah thanked God for keeping them safe. God put a beautiful rainbow in the sky to remind us of his promise to never again cover the entire world with water.

Ask:
- **Why do you think it might have been hard for Noah to obey God?**
- **When is it hard for you to obey?**
- **What happened when Noah obeyed God?**

Say: Out of all the people in the world, Noah did what was right, and God saw that Noah did right. God knows when you choose to do right, too.

Pray: **Dear God, thank you for seeing when we are doing the right things. Help us to be brave enough to always do what you ask us to do. Amen.**

Encourage children to eat their Banana Boats and Animal Crackers.

A Morsel More

✋ Play a Get-on-the-Ark game. Let two children decide together what animal to mimic. Encourage the other children to guess the animal.

✋ Place a large sheet of butcher or bulletin board paper on the wall for a mural. Have the children use old magazines and catalogs to find pictures of activities that are fun and pleasing to God. They may also use crayons or markers to draw pictures of activities that are pleasing to God.

Spice Up the Recipe!

- Instead of strawberry cream cheese, use chocolate frosting to "glue" the animal crackers together.
- Place a thin slice of strawberry or a maraschino cherry half in the center of each animal cracker sandwich along with the cream cheese or chocolate frosting.
- Coat the inside of the banana with peanut butter before placing the animals into the banana ark.
- Sprinkle the ark with chocolate chips, coconut or miniature marshmallows.
- Scoop small bits of ice cream, and press the ice cream between the two animal crackers. Freeze them until time for the Bible story. Prepare the bananas as directed on page 12, and fill them with animal ice-cream sandwiches. Drizzle chocolate sauce over the arks to represent rain.

Towers of Babel
God helps us love and understand each other.

Towers of Babel

Terrific Tools:

wax paper

snack-size resealable bags

paper plates (1 per child)

plastic knives

scissors

Fun Foods:

bananas (1 per child)

1/3 cup honey

1 cup peanut butter

1/2 cup miniature chocolate chip morsels

Before class, mix the peanut butter and honey. Put about a tablespoon of the mixture near the corner of each resealable bag and close it. Snip one-half inch off the corner of the bag near the peanut butter mix so the kids can squeeze it out.

Peel a banana, and place it on the wax paper. Cut the banana into 1/4-inch slices crosswise. Eat the two pointed ends.

Place one banana slice on a paper plate. Squeeze some peanut butter mixture onto the banana slice. Put another banana slice on top. Continue this process until the banana slices are used up.

After you have built the tower, place miniature chocolate chips around it.

The Bible Story
The Tower of Babel (Genesis 11)

Ask:

● What are some things we talk to each other about?

● Why do we talk?

● Why do we listen?

Say: When the world was still new, all the people spoke the same language. They had one word for "hello," and everyone knew what it meant. They had one word for "hungry," and everyone knew what it meant. They had one word for "stop," and everyone knew what it meant. Everyone knew what everyone else was saying.

One day the people were talking to each other. They decided to make some bricks. We're going to use banana slices to make some bricks. Give each child a banana. Have children peel the bananas and then use the plastic knives to slice them into small circles. Let children eat the two pointed ends.

The people decided to use their bricks to build a tall tower. First they placed a brick on the ground. Show children how to lay a banana slice in the center of the paper plate. Then they covered it with mortar, kind of like glue, to hold the next brick on. Show children how to squeeze some of the peanut butter mixture onto the banana slice and then lay another banana slice on top. **They wanted their tower to be the tallest tower in the world.** Have the kids keep building until they run out of banana slices, as you continue talking. **They wanted their tower to be so tall that it would reach up to heaven. They wanted everyone who saw the tower to think that they were the greatest people in the whole world.**

God was not pleased with the people's tower. God knew they were thinking too much about themselves. God knew they were forgetting that they needed him. So God gave them many different languages, maybe even more languages than the chocolate chips I'm giving you! Hand out miniature chocolate chip morsels to the children.

Now when one man asked for a hammer, the others did not know what he wanted. Have the children begin placing chocolate chips around their towers. **When another man asked for a brick, no one else knew what he wanted. They could not understand each other anymore. They had to stop building their tower because they couldn't work together.** Ask:

● Have you ever heard people speaking to each other in a language you didn't understand? What did it sound like?

● How can we help someone who doesn't understand our words?

Pray: Dear God, when we treat each other with your love and kindness everyone understands. Help us to remember that in all we say and do we should show your love to those around us. Amen.

A Morsel More

🖐 Learn American Sign Language for the words to the song "Jesus Loves Me."

🖐 Play a modified form of charades. Whisper a simple activity, such as setting the table, picking up toys, climbing a tree, jumping rope, or having a tea party. After you whisper to each child, let him or her act out the task. The rest of the class can try to guess what the child is acting out!

Spice Up the Recipe!

● Place your banana tower in a bowl; top it with your favorite chocolate sauce, whipped cream, and a cherry half; and you have a Babbling Banana Sundae.

Pita Pouches
We can follow God wherever he leads us.

Pita Pouches

Terrific Tools:

knife

measuring cups

spoon

cutting board

paper towels

Fun Foods:

mayonnaise (1 teaspoon per child)

pita bread halves, cut open (1 per child)

luncheon meat slices (1 per child)

carrot sticks (2 per child)

lettuce leaves, washed and dried (1 per child)

Use a carrot stick to spread the mayonnaise on one side of the pita pocket. Place the lettuce leaf on the mayonnaise-coated side of the pita bread. Place the luncheon meat on the lettuce. Place two carrot sticks in the pita pouch, and serve.

The Bible Story
Abram and Sarai Follow God (Genesis 16)

Ask:

● How does it feel to trust someone?

● Who do you trust? Who trusts you?

Say: Abram and Sarai lived in a place called Haran (HAY-ran). One day God asked Abram to take Sarai and leave their home and their friends and family and go to a land God would show them. God promised that he would make Abram's family a great nation. God promised that he would do good to those who did good to Abram. Abram and Sarai didn't know where this land God promised them would be. They didn't know how far away it was or what it would be like. But they did know God, and they trusted God to lead and take care of them.

So Abram and Sarai packed all their belongings. Give each child a pita. Maybe they spread everything out on the ground. Take a carrot stick, and spread mayonnaise on the inside of your suitcase bread. Then you can pack in some lettuce, carrots, and luncheon meat. Give kids a chance to pack their pitas. When they had finished packing, they left their home, their families, and their friends and followed God.

Abram and Sarai weren't sure where God would lead them, but they knew they could trust God. Ask:

● What are some things you would take if you were going to leave your home?

● How would you feel if you weren't sure you would have toys or good food where you were going?

● Who do you trust to give you what you need?

● Who did Abram trust to get him what he needed?

Pray: **Dear God, thank you for the people you have given us to provide for our needs. Thank you that we can always trust you, wherever we go. Amen.**

Enjoy your packed Pita Pouches!

A Morsel More

Form pairs. Blindfold one child in each pair. Ask the other child to lead the blindfolded partner to find something, such as a special treat or a sticker. Let the partners switch roles. Talk about how this experience is like trusting God when we can't see or understand.

Switch the red and yellow lids on red and yellow food coloring. Hold up the bottle containing yellow coloring (which now has the red lid). Ask the kids what color is in the bottle. Tell the kids that it is yellow. Let them look at the fluid and the lid. Tell them that even though it looks as though it is red, they can trust you that it is really yellow. Put several drops into a glass of water. Say: Even though it looked as though it was red, you discovered that you could trust what I told you. Talk about how we can trust God's Word because God knows everything.

Spice Up the Recipe!

● Stuff the pita pocket with anything from homemade tuna salad to peanut butter and jelly. Try mixing favorite lettuces, carrots, tomato, and bacon crumbles with a little ranch dressing, and fill the pita with the salad.

Coat of Many Colors Sandwiches

We should be careful not to let angry feelings lead to wrong choices.

Coat of Many Colors Sandwiches

Terrific Tools:

paper plates

plastic knives

3 squirt bottles

Fun Foods:

white bread (2 slices per child)   peanut butter (2 tablespoons per child)

grape, strawberry, and apricot jellies in squirt bottles (2 tablespoons per child)

Before class, cut the crusts off of the bread, and cut each piece into a coat shape.

Spread each coat with a layer of peanut butter. Squirt on lines of each color of jelly.

(From Group Publishing, Inc.'s *Incredible Edible Bible Story Fun for Preschoolers;*
copyright © 1999 Jane C. Jarrell and Deborah L. Saathoff.)

The Bible Story

Joseph and His Coat (Genesis 37)

Ask:

● Have you ever been very angry with someone? Why?

● What unkind things do people do when they're angry?

Say: Today we're going to hear about someone in the Bible whose brothers were very angry with him. Because they acted in anger, they did things that hurt God, their father, and their brother. But God turned their hateful actions into something good.

Jacob had twelve sons, but he loved Joseph more than the others. Jacob gave Joseph a special present, a coat. **Give each child a bread "coat" on a paper plate. We don't know exactly what Joseph's coat looked like, but the Bible tells us it had many colors. Maybe it had a brown background. Let's spread some peanut butter over the bread to make a brown background.** Let the kids spread the peanut butter themselves. **Maybe the many colors were stripes over the brown background. Let's take turns squirting on these different colors of jelly.** Show the kids how to squirt on lines of jelly.

As they work, say: Joseph's brothers did not like him. They never said a kind word to him. They were very jealous of Joseph's new coat. Maybe they wanted new coats too. Joseph's brothers were very angry.

One night Joseph had a dream. He told his brothers, "We were gathering grain in my dream. My bundle of grain stood up, and your bundles of grain bowed down to mine." It was kind of like saying, "In my dream, I was the best brother of all!"

Joseph's brothers did not like this dream. It made them angry. They couldn't stand the idea of bowing down to their little brother.

Joseph had more dreams. The brothers got angrier and angrier. Finally, they decided to get rid of Joseph. They took his coat away from him. Then they sold him to some traders who were traveling to far away places. After he was gone, they messed up Joseph's coat so it looked as though a wild animal had attacked him. Have the kids put the top piece of bread on and smash it down so that the jelly stripes get messed up. Let them open the sandwich to see what happened. When their father saw the coat, he thought Joseph was dead, and he was very sad.

The traders took Joseph to Egypt. But God was with Joseph. God was watching over him, and he had a special plan for Joseph in Egypt. God can use even the bad things that happen to us for good. Taste your coat sandwich, and see how good it is.

Say: Joseph's brothers let their anger cause them to make wrong choices. Ask:

● What are some things we can do when we feel angry so that we don't hurt ourselves or the people around us?

Pray: Dear God, help us make careful decisions when we feel angry so that we don't hurt you or others with our words or actions. Amen.

A Morsel More

✋ Make a giant coat! Don't remove the crusts from the bread. Let each child spread the peanut butter and squeeze jelly stripes on a full piece of bread. Then place six slices of bread in two columns (sides touching). Place two more pieces of bread (one on each side) to form the sleeves.

✋ Call out an emotion, and have the children make a face that expresses that emotion. (Happy, sad, angry, frightened, worried, and surprised are all possibilities.)

✋ Use paper plates and crayons to make faces that show different emotions. Talk about things that make us feel those emotions. Discuss positive actions that can be used to express each emotion. With each one, stress that we can always talk to God about what we feel and why we feel that way.

Spice Up the Recipe!

● Use wheat bread as the "coat," and spread it with a soft cheese. Cut strips of turkey, ham, and roast beef, and use them for the stripes on the coat.

● Cut a coat shape out of a piece of poundcake. Spread the poundcake "coat" with a thin layer of icing, and use miniature chocolate chip morsels, butterscotch morsels, and white chocolate or peanut butter morsels to make the stripes.

Joseph's Granola Bags
God wants us to forgive others.

Joseph's Granola Bags

Terrific Tools:

measuring cups

1 large spoon

scissors

1 large bowl

small brown paper bags (1 per child)

twine (5 inches per child)

Fun Foods:

3 cups granola

1/2 cup raisins

1 cup frosted wheat cereal

Place all ingredients in a large bowl; stir to combine. Using a measuring cup, scoop equal amounts of Joseph's granola into several brown paper bags. Cut 5-inch pieces of twine, and tie each bag.

(From Group Publishing, Inc.'s *Incredible Edible Bible Story Fun for Preschoolers*; copyright © 1999 Jane C. Jarrell and Deborah L. Saathoff.)

The Bible Story
Joseph Forgives His Brothers (Genesis 45)

Ask:

● Have you forgiven someone? How did it make you feel?

● Has anyone ever forgiven you? How did it feel to be forgiven?

Say: Joseph became a great ruler in Egypt. With God's help, he had told the king what an important dream meant. The king's dream warned that seven years of good crops and plenty of food would be followed by seven years when no food would grow. Because he knew this, the king put Joseph in charge of saving food during the years of plenty so no one would be hungry during the seven bad years. Ask a child to pour one cup of granola into the bowl, ask another to pour in the wheat cereal, and ask a third to pour in the raisins. Have the rest of the children take turns stirring as you talk about the different kinds of food Joseph may have stored.

People in Canaan didn't know about the warning. When the food stopped growing, they didn't have any food. But they had heard about all the food saved in Egypt. So Joseph's brothers went to Egypt to try to buy some.

When they got to Egypt, Joseph's brothers bowed down to him and asked him for some food. They didn't know he was their brother. But Joseph knew who they were. Joseph sold them some food, but he didn't tell them he was their brother. Give each child a tiny bit of the granola, and have the children eat all that you give them.

It wasn't long until Joseph's brothers needed more food. They had to go back to Egypt. Again they bowed down to Joseph and asked him for food.

This time Joseph told his brothers who he was. His brothers were afraid of him because they had treated him badly and now he was a powerful ruler.

But Joseph told them, "Don't be afraid. God sent me here so I could save your lives." He kissed his brothers and sent them home with more food. Allow each child to place some granola in a brown paper bag.

Joseph's brothers went home and told their father that Joseph was alive and ruling in Egypt. The whole family moved to Egypt to be close to Joseph. Joseph had shown forgiveness to his brothers by being kind to them. Ask:

- Why do you think Joseph forgave his brothers?
- How can we show that we forgive someone?

Say: God wants us to forgive others even when they have done something mean to us. We can show our forgiveness by being kind.

Pray: Dear God, thank you for forgiving us when we do things that make you sad. Please help us to show your forgiveness to others when they hurt us. Amen.

A Morsel More

☝ Joseph explained to his brothers that even though what they had done was meant to harm him, God used it for good. Illustrate this idea by making some recycled art. Gather materials that are typically thrown away, such as toilet paper tubes or paper towel tubes, cereal boxes and other cardboard boxes, scraps of construction paper, old magazines, milk cartons and their caps, yogurt cups and lids, egg cartons, foil, and grocery bags. Allow the students to use the items, along with tape, scissors, and glue, to create their own art from what would have been trash.

☝ Use a magnetic drawing screen to illustrate how God forgives us. Make marks or designs on the clean screen to represent the mistakes we've made and the sins we've committed. Erase the design, showing the clean screen again, to demonstrate that when we tell God the wrong things we have done, he forgives us and never remembers our sins again.

Spice Up the Recipe!

- Be creative with the ingredients you place in the bags. You can add candy corn, popcorn, chocolate candies, trail mix, dried bananas, or other dried fruit.

Baby Bread Baskets

God protects us.

Baby Bread Baskets

Terrific Tools:

plates (1 per child)   plastic knives

Fun Foods:

oval-shaped dinner rolls (1 per child)   American cheese slices (1 per child)

grapes (1 per child)   stick pretzels (2 per child)

thinly sliced ham (1 slice per child)

Before class, hollow out each dinner roll so that it resembles a basket.
Roll a cheese slice so that it resembles a baby in a blanket. Push a grape into one end of the cheese to form the baby's head. Push pretzels into the cheese on either side to form arms. Place the baby in the bread basket. Cover the baby with a blanket of thinly sliced ham.

(From Group Publishing, Inc.'s *Incredible Edible Bible Story Fun for Preschoolers;*
copyright © 1999 Jane C. Jarrell and Deborah L. Saathoff.)

The Bible Story

Moses in the Basket (Exodus 2)

Ask:

● What does it mean to protect?

● Who protects you?

Say: The Bible tells us how a special baby was protected. His name was Moses. Moses' parents, along with all the other Israelites, were slaves in Egypt. They had to work very hard for the Egyptians.

The new king worried that if more and more Israelites were born, there would be more Israelites than there were Egyptians. He did not like that idea. He was a very mean king, and he made an awful new rule that said that any Israelite baby boys would have to be killed. Show the children how to roll the cheese and put the grape in at the top. Show them how to add the pretzel arms. Then give each child a paper plate, a slice of cheese, a grape, and two pretzels. Help each one make a baby Moses.

Moses' mother hid her baby boy for three months, but then she realized she couldn't hide him any longer. She found a large basket and sealed it with tar so that no water could get inside. Give each child a hollowed out roll.

The woman placed her baby inside the basket. Have the children put their babies inside the bread. She covered him with his blanket. Lay a slice of ham over each baby. Then she carried the basket to the river. She put the basket into the water, and it began to float. The baby's sister stayed near the river to watch what would happen.

The king's daughter went to the river to take a bath. She saw the basket floating in the river and sent one of her slaves to get it for her. When she looked in the basket, she saw the baby. He was crying, and she felt very sorry for him. She knew he was an Israelite baby.

The baby's sister asked the princess, "Would you like me to find someone to help you take care of the baby?" The princess said yes, so the baby's sister ran to get their mother. The king's daughter asked the baby's mother to take care of the baby for her. The princess named him Moses. When he got older, he lived with the princess in the king's palace. Ask:

● How did God protect Moses?

● How do you help protect others?

Pray: Dear God, thank you for giving us the people in our lives who help protect us and keep us safe. Amen.

Enjoy your Baby Bread Baskets!

A Morsel More

✋ The Bible includes many instructions for taking care of God's creation. For example, we are to take care of our pets: "A righteous man cares for the needs of his animal" (Proverbs 12:10a). We are to care for lost animals: "If you see your brother's ox or sheep straying, do not ignore it but be sure to take it back to him" (Deuteronomy 22:1). And we are to care for animals who are injured: "If you see your brother's donkey or his ox fallen on the road, do not ignore it. Help him get it to its feet" (Deuteronomy 22:4). Talk about the ways children have cared for animals.

✋ Talk about rules that help keep us safe.

✋ Form two groups. Give each child a Ping-Pong ball and each team a plastic spoon. Put two containers at one end of the room, the children at the other. Instruct each child to carry his or her Ping-Pong ball on the spoon from one end of the room to the container at the other end. Tell children to try to go quickly but to protect the Ping-Pong balls from falling by moving carefully!

Spice Up the Recipe!

● Spread peanut butter around the insides of the hollowed-out bread basket. Then fill the basket with jelly, and add a dried fruit "baby."

Burning Bushes

God helps us when we are afraid.

Burning Bushes

Terrific Tools:

plastic knives   paper plates

Fun Foods:

rice cakes (1 per child)   strawberry preserves (2 tablespoons per child)

Using a small plastic knife, spread a layer of preserves over the rice cake

(From Group Publishing, Inc.'s *Incredible Edible Bible Story Fun for Preschoolers*; copyright © 1999 Jane C. Jarrell and Deborah L. Saathoff.)

The Bible Story
Moses and the Burning Bush (Exodus 3)

Ask:

● When have you felt afraid?

Say: I'm going to tell you about a time Moses felt afraid. Moses didn't like the way the pharaoh treated the Israelites, so when he grew up, he went to live in another country. He took care of sheep. He stayed with the sheep out in fields with grass and bushes all around.

One day while Moses was watching the sheep, he noticed a bush. It was a plain bush, kind of like these rice cakes are plain and ordinary. Hand out the rice cakes on paper plates. But this time the bush was very different—it was on fire! Let's spread some red jam on top of the rice cakes to help us think about the bush being on fire. Let the children use plastic knives to spread the preserves.

What made this even more unusual was that the bush never burned up. It just stayed on fire, burning and burning. The fire sat on the bush just as this jam is sitting on the rice cake.

Moses went closer to get a better look. When he was very close, Moses heard God's voice coming from the burning bush. "Moses! I want you to go to the king. Tell him to let my people leave Egypt."

Moses was very frightened. The king was very powerful and would not like what God wanted Moses to say.

God promised to be with Moses. Even though he was frightened, Moses believed God. He went back to Egypt just as God had told him to.

Moses had courage. Courage doesn't mean you're not frightened. Courage means doing what is right even when you are frightened. And God promises us he is always with us. Whatever we do, God is right beside us, just as he was beside Moses. Ask:

● When do you need to know God is beside you?

Pray: **Dear God, sometimes we have to do things that are new and scary. Help us to remember that you are with us and will help us do the things you tell us to do. Amen.**

Encourage the children to eat their Burning Bushes.

A Morsel More

✋ Help the kids memorize a Scripture verse to remember when they are frightened, such as part of Hebrews 13:6: "The Lord is my helper; I will not be afraid."

✋ Interview people in your congregation who are in careers that require unusual courage, such as missions, law enforcement, firefighting, and the military.

Spice Up the Recipe!

● Add fresh strawberries to the Burning Bushes.

● Spread a soft cheese over the top of the rice cake, and cover it with a slice of turkey and bacon crumbles.

Red Sea Surprise
God can help us in amazing ways!

Red Sea Surprise

Terrific Tools:

a 13x9x2-inch pan

1 spatula

plastic spoons

1 large spoon

serving cups (1 per child)

Fun Foods:

1 small package miniature marshmallows

1 eight-ounce container nondairy whipped topping

1 six-pack prepared red gelatin snack cups

Combine gelatin snack cups and nondairy whipped topping in a 13x9x2-inch pan. Break the gelatin up into small pieces as you stir. Stir marshmallows into the gelatin mixture. Mix well before serving.

(From Group Publishing, Inc.'s *Incredible Edible Bible Story Fun for Preschoolers*; copyright © 1999 Jane C. Jarrell and Deborah L. Saathoff.)

The Bible Story
Moses and the Israelites Cross the Red Sea (Exodus 13–14)

Ask:

● What are some things God can do?

Say: **God can do all kinds of things that people can't do! For example, when Moses and the Israelites were leaving Egypt, God helped them know exactly where to go. During the day, God led the way with a pillar of clouds that might have looked like a stack of these marshmallows.** Let the children try to stack the marshmallows.

God led the Israelites to a place beside the Red Sea. Let's make a red sea. Let several children empty the gelatin cups into the baking pan. Break the gelatin up with a spoon. **Now let's put some waves into our red sea.** Spoon in the whipped topping. Let the kids take turns stirring the swirling waters.

While the Israelites were near the Red Sea, the Egyptian king decided he wanted them to come back and be his slaves again. He sent his army after the Israelites to capture them and bring them back to Egypt. The Israelites looked behind them and saw the soldiers. They looked in front of them and saw the Red Sea. They didn't know what to do! If they let the soldiers catch them, they'd be slaves again. If they went into the Red Sea, they'd drown!

But Moses told them not to be afraid. He told them God would take care of them, even if it looked impossible. That night a strong wind blew. It blew so hard and so long that it pushed the waters of the sea apart. Use the spatula to separate your red sea. Make sure you scrape it across the bottom to form a clean, clear path.

God's people were able to walk across the bottom of the sea and get to the land on the other side. Let the children walk their fingers across the space you created.

The Egyptian army saw the Israelites walk across the sea on dry ground. They tried to follow the Israelites to capture them on the other side. Here comes the

army...Ask a child to pour the miniature marshmallows into the pan. Shake the pan as you explain: **The water covered all of the Egyptian army. But God's people were safe on the other side.** Stir the marshmallows into the mixture, and serve it up in cups.

When the people couldn't figure out how to solve their problem, God helped them in an amazing way. The Israelites were so happy they sang a song of thanks to God. Ask:

● **What problems has God helped you or your family to solve?**

Pray: **Dear God, thank you for helping us solve problems in amazing ways. Help us to trust you to do what you say, even if things look impossible to us. Amen.**

A Morsel More

 Re-examine "everyday miracles" to remind the children that God does amazing things all the time. We see them so often that we sometimes forget the wonder of them. Gather magnifying glasses, and take the children on a nature walk. Look for bugs and butterflies. Examine flowers and leaves. Bring seashells for children to examine in class.

Have a large tub, basin, or water table available. Let the children try to "part the waters" as they play.

Spice Up the Recipe!

● Add chopped nuts, mandarin oranges, or any other fruits to the Red Sea Surprise.

● Pour the mixture into a prepared graham cracker crust, and freeze overnight. Slice into wedges, and serve with nondairy whipped topping.

Marvelous Manna
God will provide for us.

Marvelous Manna

Terrific Tools:

1 large airtight plastic container	1 liquid measuring cup
measuring spoons	spoons
serving cups (1 per child)	

Fun Foods:

1 six-ounce package vanilla pudding mix	3 cups milk
1/3 cup puffed rice cereal	1 teaspoon honey
1/4 teaspoon cinnamon	

Prepare pudding as directed on the package. Add the remaining ingredients, and stir to combine.

(From Group Publishing, Inc.'s *Incredible Edible Bible Story Fun for Preschoolers*;
copyright © 1999 Jane C. Jarrell and Deborah L. Saathoff.)

The Bible Story
Moses and the Israelites Find Manna (Exodus 16)

Ask:

● What does it mean to complain?

● Is it OK to complain? Why or why not?

Say: Let's talk about some people who complained. The Israelites had come out of slavery in Egypt carrying treasures. They had seen God make the waters of the Red Sea move apart so they could cross the sea on dry land, and they had seen many other miracles.

These were good things. Let's mix some good things, like milk and this special powder, to remind us of the good things the Israelites carried with them. Put the milk and the pudding mix in the airtight container. **But instead of thanking God and praising him for the good things, the Israelites complained.** Let the children take turns shaking the container. Have the children hand it to a classmate at each new statement. **They whined.** Shake. **They griped.** Shake. **They fussed.** Shake. **They said God brought them out of Egypt to let them die in the wilderness.** Shake. **They said they wanted to go back to Egypt.** Shake **They said they wanted to be slaves again.** Shake. **They said they were hungry.** Shake. **They said that God wasn't taking care of them.** Shake. Shake. Shake. Make sure you have shaken the contents enough to form the pudding.

The more they complained, the harder their lives got. See how hard this mixture is getting? Remove the lid from the container. **The Israelites did not trust God to take care of them even after all they had seen him do. But God told Moses that God would send special bread from heaven. He would not let the people go hungry.**

The next morning the Israelites found small white flakes lying all over the ground. Ask a child to add the cereal to the pudding. Moses told them that this was the bread God had given them to eat. The Israelites tasted it. It tasted like wafers made with honey. Ask a child to add the honey to the pudding.

God said each family was to gather as much as it would need to eat that day. Ask a child to add the cinnamon to the pudding. Then pour the mixture into cups.

The bread from heaven appeared every morning. And every morning the Israelites gathered enough food for the entire day. Even though the Israelites complained, God gave them good things to show his love for them. Ask:

● What do you think the Israelites should have done instead of complaining?

● In the Bible, Philippians 2:14 tells us, "Do everything without complaining or arguing." What can we do when we feel like complaining? Discuss the children's ideas.

Pray: **Dear God, help us to remember to be cheerful and to trust you. Help us to remember all of the good things you do for us and to talk about those things to everyone we meet. Amen.**

Enjoy this Marvelous Manna snack with the children.

A Morsel More

🖐 Make a "Good Things Book." Give each child a large piece of paper. Provide crayons, markers, or pictures cut from magazines, and have the children put a picture on each page of something to be happy about or thankful for. Assemble all the pages into a class book, and put it where the children can look through it. Talk about how the book they made helps them think about good things.

🖐 Write each child's name on a piece of paper. Put the papers into a container. Ask the children to sit in a circle and have each child draw a name from the container; then read it to him or her. If a child draws his or her own name, have the child return it to the container and draw again. Ask each child to say something kind about the person whose name he or she drew.

🖐 Sing "If You're Happy and You Know It."

Spice Up the Recipe!
● Make chocolate pudding, and mix in miniature marshmallows.
● Make butterscotch pudding, and stir in honey-roasted nuts.

Commandment Cakes
God wants us to obey his laws.

Commandment Cakes

Terrific Tools:

1 cutting board	1 knife
cookie cutters of the numbers zero through nine	10 large paper plates
small paper plates (1 per child)	plastic knives
plastic forks (1 per child)	

Fun Foods:

1 prepared poundcake for every 10 kids	frosting
cake- and-cookie decorating sprinkles	

Before class, cut a poundcake into 11 slices.
Using the cookie cutters, cut numbers one through ten from the poundcake. Decorate the cake numbers with frosting and decorating sprinkles.

The Bible Story
The Ten Commandments (Exodus 20)

Ask:
- What rules do you have to follow?
- How did you learn about those rules?

Say: Those are some good rules. Rules help us live together safely and in peace. God wanted the Israelites to live together safely and in peace, so one day God called Moses to the top of a mountain and gave him rules for the Israelites to follow. The rules were so important that God wrote them on stone that would last a *long* time. In fact, he wanted his people to never forget these rules. Set out slices of poundcake. God wrote ten rules we call the Ten Commandments. Set out number cookie cutters. **Listen to those commandments:**

1. **Don't worship anyone or anything but God.** Let a child use the cookie cutter to cut the number one.

2. **Don't make statues of gods to worship.** Ask a child to cut out the number two.

3. **Use God's name in the right way.** Ask a child to cut out the number three.

4. **Remember to set aside one day each week to rest and honor God.** Ask a child to cut out the number four.

5. **Honor your mother and your father.** Ask a child to cut out the number five.

Say: **Let's count how many we have so far...**Point to each number as you count together. **Is that all the commandments God gave? No, there are several more!**

6. **Don't kill anyone.** Ask a child to cut out the number six.

7. **Be true to your husband or wife.** Ask a child to cut out the number seven.

8. **Don't steal.** Ask a child to cut out the number eight.

9. **Don't lie.** Ask a child to cut out the number nine.

10. **Don't want something that belongs to someone else.** Ask two children to cut out the numbers one and zero. Place them together to make ten.

Say: **Let's count now!** Point to each numeral as you count. Ask:

● **Why do you think God gave his people Ten Commandments?**

Let's see if you can remember ten kinds of animals. I'll keep track while you tell me. Count on your fingers as the children name ten animals.

Let's see if you can remember ten different toys. I'll keep track again. Count on your fingers as children name toys.

Say: **These rules are easy to remember once we learn them.** Ask:

● **What do you think God wants us to do with these rules?**

● **What do you think would happen if people didn't have rules?**

Pray: **Dear God, you gave us rules to help us get along with each other and with you. Help us to obey the rules you have given. Amen.**

Give each child a cake number. (Cut more if necessary.) Let children spread frosting on the numbers, and sprinkle them with decorations.

A Morsel More

✋ Have kids talk about the rules for your class. Ask them how these rules are like the Ten Commandments and how they are different?

✋ Play a simple game your kids already know how to play, such as Red Light, Green Light. Ask the kids what rules they noticed during the game and what would happen if somebody decided not to play by the rules. Ask how they would feel about someone else not playing by the rules. Ask how they would feel about not following the rules themselves.

Spice Up the Recipe!

● Cut wheat bread in the shapes of numbers one through ten. Using a canned cheese or cheese in a tube, put one dot on the number one, two dots on the number two, and so on.

Cherry-Ball Wall
God wants us to obey people in charge.

Cherry-Ball Wall

Terrific Tools:

1 large plastic bag	1 rolling pin
1 large bowl	1 spoon
1 teaspoon	wax paper

Fun Foods:

1 box vanilla wafers	1 small can frozen cherry juice, thawed
1 box powdered sugar	

Before class, crush wafers in a large plastic bag by rolling over them with a rolling pin until they are finely crushed. In a large bowl, combine crushed wafers, cherry juice, and powdered sugar. Stir thoroughly to combine. Scoop out the dough with a teaspoon, roll it into balls, and then flatten it slightly to look like stones. Use the balls to build a wall.

(From Group Publishing, Inc.'s *Incredible Edible Bible Story Fun for Preschoolers;*
copyright © 1999 Jane C. Jarrell and Deborah L. Saathoff.)

The Bible Story
Joshua and the Wall of Jericho (Joshua 6)

Ask:
- Who do you have to obey?
- Who do your parents have to obey?

Say: **God's people had a new leader named Joshua. They had to learn to obey him. Joshua led God's people to the land God had promised them. The first city they came to was Jericho. It had a big wall around it, and the people who lived there would not let God's people inside. Let's build a wall like the one that surrounded Jericho.** Working as a group around a table or desk, cover the surface with wax paper. Use a teaspoon to scoop out a little of the mixture, and allow children each to roll a scoop into a ball and then flatten it slightly to resemble a rock. Repeat this process until the mixture is used up. Ask the children to stack a layer of rocks in a circle. Then build the wall several levels high.

As the children work, say: **The wall went all around the city of Jericho. It made the people who lived there feel safe. But the people didn't know that God had sent a message to Joshua that the Israelites were supposed to live in the city of Jericho. God wanted Joshua and his soldiers to march around the walls of Jericho once a day for six days.**

On the seventh day, Joshua and his army were to march around the city seven times. The seventh time they circled the city, the priests were to blow their horns, and the people were to shout. When they did these things, God would do something amazing.

Joshua obeyed God. The people of Israel obeyed Joshua. They gathered together to get ready to march.

The first day Joshua and his men walked around the city of Jericho. Have the children march around the table one time.

The second day Joshua and his men walked around the city of Jericho. Have them march around again for each day you mention.

The third day Joshua and his men walked around the city.

The fourth day they did it again.

The fifth day they did it again.

The sixth day they did it again.

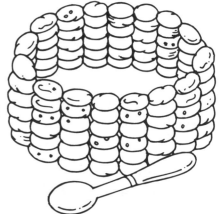

The seventh day was an exciting one for Joshua and the people of Israel. They marched around the city seven times. As a group, walk around the table.

The seventh time they walked, the priests blew their horns, and the people shouted. Have children shout and pretend to blow horns. And the walls came tumbling down. Shake the table until your "stones" fall down. Ask:

● Who did Joshua obey? Who did the Israelites obey?

● What might have happened if they hadn't obeyed?

Pray: Dear God, we thank you for being in charge of our world. Help us to obey you, and help us to obey those you have chosen to lead us. May they look to you for their guidance, and may we obey the instructions they give us. Amen.

A Morsel More

🖑 Play Simon Says.

🖑 Play Mother, May I? Mark a starting line and a finish line. One player is designated "Mother" and stands at the finish line. All other players line up at the starting line. Mother tells the players one at a time how to move closer to Mother: a baby step (one foot-length), a giant step (the longest step the player can make), a hop (a hopping step on one foot), or a bunny hop (a hop with both feet together). After being told how to move ("Lauren, you may take one giant step"), Lauren must answer, "Mother, may I?" Mother answers, "You may." Then Lauren may take her giant step. If she forgets to ask, "Mother, may I?" she must go back to the starting line. The first player to reach Mother is the winner.

Spice Up the Recipe!

● Mix your favorite kind of juice (orange, cranberry, or grape) with the wafers and sugar.

● Add nuts, raisins, or chocolate chips to the mixture.

Ruth's Wheat Bundles
God wants us to help other people.

Ruth's Wheat Bundles

Terrific Tools:

measuring cups

brown paper bags (1 per child)

1 cookie sheet

twine (5 inches per child)

Fun Foods:

1 box frosted wheat squares cereal

2 cups raisin bran cereal

Pour the box of frosted wheat squares onto a cookie sheet. Add the raisin bran. Partially fill a brown paper bag with the wheat and raisin bran mix. Tie the bag with twine.

(From Group Publishing, Inc.'s *Incredible Edible Bible Story Fun for Preschoolers*; copyright © 1999 Jane C. Jarrell and Deborah L. Saathoff.)

The Bible Story
Ruth Gathers Grain (Ruth 1)

Ask:

● What do you do to help other people?

Say: In the Bible, a woman named Ruth lived in a country far away from Judah, the land of God's people. She lived with her husband's mother, Naomi, but her husband had died. Naomi wanted to go back to Judah, where she had lived when she was a little girl. Ruth wanted to go with her. "Please take me with you," she told Naomi. "I will go where you go and live where you live. I will worship your God with you."

So Naomi and Ruth went to Judah together. Ruth had to work very hard to get food so she and Naomi could eat. When workers picked the grain in the fields (ask a child to pour the box of frosted wheat squares onto the cookie sheet), Ruth would go to the field and pick up the grain that was left on the ground. Explain to children that cereal has grain in it.

The owner of the field was named Boaz (BOH-az). He watched Ruth picking up the grain. He knew she was working hard to help Naomi. He told his workers to leave extra grain especially for Ruth. Ask a child to pour the raisin bran onto the cookie sheet with the wheat squares.

Boaz was glad Ruth was gathering grain in his field. He wanted to help her as she worked to help Naomi. Ruth knew that Boaz was a kind man.

He made sure that Ruth had plenty of grain to take back to Naomi. Ask the children to put some of the mixture into the paper bags. Ask:

Ask:

● Did Ruth have to help Naomi? Did Boaz have to help Ruth? Why did they do it?

● When could you help someone without being asked?

Pray: Dear God, thank you for sending people who help us when we need it. Help us to find ways to help other people too. Amen.

Say: You may eat your Wheat Bundles now or take them to share with someone else.

A Morsel More

✋ As a class service project, ask the children to bring clothing, food, books, or toys for less fortunate families. If possible, arrange for the children to accompany you when you deliver the material. Explain to the children that when we help someone in Jesus' name, Jesus says we are helping him.

Spice Up the Recipe!

● Make a brown bag lunch. Pack a small loaf of wheat bread, some fruit (such as an apple, a banana, or a pear), and a small wedge of cheese. Tie the bag with twine, and give it to someone who needs help.

Tortilla Bedrolls

God helps us listen.

Tortilla Bedrolls

Terrific Tools:

plastic knives

plates (1 per child)

toothpicks (1 per child)

Fun Foods:

tortillas (1 per child)

thinly sliced ham (1 per child)

softened cream cheese, 2 tablespoons per child

slices of American cheese (1 slice per child)

Place a tortilla on a plate. Spread a thin layer of cream cheese on the tortilla. Place a ham slice on top of the cream cheese. Place a cheese slice on top of the ham. Roll up the tortilla, and secure it with the toothpick.

(From Group Publishing, Inc.'s *Incredible Edible Bible Story Fun for Preschoolers*; copyright © 1999 Jane C. Jarrell and Deborah L. Saathoff.)

The Bible Story

Samuel Listens to God (1 Samuel 3)

Ask:

● When is it hard to listen to someone?

● When has someone said something that surprised you?

Say: Samuel was a boy who lived at the Temple, which was like church, and helped Eli the priest. One night after they had gone to bed, Samuel heard a voice call him. He ran to Eli. "Here I am," Samuel said.

But Eli hadn't called Samuel, so he sent him back to bed. Let's make a bedroll like the one Samuel might have slept in. Give each child a plate containing a tortilla topped with cream cheese. Have children use plastic knives to spread the cream cheese.

Soon Samuel heard the voice call his name again. He got up and went to Eli. "Here I am," Samuel said.

"I didn't call you," Eli said. "Go back to bed." So Samuel went back to bed and pulled up his blanket. Have children place a thin slice of ham on each tortilla.

Once again Samuel heard someone call, "Samuel! Samuel!" And one more time he went to Eli.

This time Eli realized that God must be calling Samuel. Eli told Samuel to lie down again. "If you hear the voice again," Eli said, "say, 'Speak Lord, I am listening.'"

Samuel went back to his bed, pulled up both his covers, and listened. Have children each place a cheese slice on top of the ham. Again he heard, "Samuel! Samuel!"

This time, Samuel answered as Eli had told him: "Speak Lord, for I am listening."

God spoke to Samuel. He told Samuel that he would grow up to be an important prophet. He would tell God's people the things God wanted them to know. Samuel was surprised by what God told him. Everything happened just as God

told Samuel it would. Have children roll up the tortillas, and help them to secure them with toothpicks. Ask:

- **Why do you think Samuel didn't know who was calling him?**
- **How did Eli know it was God's voice?**
- **How do you listen to God?**

Pray: **Dear God, help us learn to hear your voice. Amen.**

A Morsel More

👋 Use a tape recorder to record each child saying a simple message, such as "God loves you" or "God talks to us through the Bible." Play back the tape, and see if the children recognize their voices. Children will be surprised at how different their voices sound on tape.

👋 Make or buy an audiotape of familiar sounds, such as a doorbell, a telephone, rain, wind, thunder, traffic, birds singing, dogs barking, footsteps, glass breaking, water running, or a timer buzzing. Play the tape, and see how many sounds the children can identify.

👋 Play Listening Tag. Mark off a corner of the room or an area outdoors. (The more children in your class, the larger the play area should be.) Blindfold all the players except "It." Give "It" a noisemaker, such as a bell or tambourine. "It" arranges all the players around the border of the play area, keeping the noisemaker quiet. Then "It" chooses a position and shakes the noisemaker. Now the other players can begin looking for "It." Anytime "It" moves, he or she must shake the noisemaker. "It" must stay within the border of the play area. Whoever tags "It" gets to be "It" in the next round.

Spice Up the Recipe!

- Roll any meat or vegetable into the tortilla. Try spreading the tortilla with herbed cheese (or leftover mashed potatoes!), and top it with roast beef. Roll it tightly, and have an adult help to slice the tortilla roll into one-half inch, bite-sized appetizers. They'll look like little edible ears!

Happy Harps
We can thank God with music.

Happy Harps

Terrific Tools:

plastic knives

plates (1 per child)

Fun Foods:

large pretzels (1 per child)

string cheese (1 per child)

Select a large, well-formed pretzel. Separate the string cheese into thin sections to resemble harp strings. Wrap the cheese strings around either end of the pretzel to look like a harp.

(From Group Publishing, Inc.'s *Incredible Edible Bible Story Fun for Preschoolers*; copyright © 1999 Jane C. Jarrell and Deborah L. Saathoff.)

Bible Story

David Plays His Harp (1 Samuel 16)

Ask:

● What makes you feel better when you feel sad?

Say: When King Saul felt sad, his servants thought that harp music would help him feel better. Hand each child a pretzel.

They found out that a shepherd boy named David could play beautiful harp music. Hand each child a piece of string cheese. **Harps have strings. Can you tear your cheese apart to make some strings for a harp?** Have each child separate the cheese into thin "harp strings." **David knew many songs. He sang songs about God.** Have the children each wrap a string around each end of the pretzel. **These songs helped to calm Saul when he was upset.** Have the children each wrap one more string around the pretzel. **David's harp probably looked a lot like the one you just made.**

● Why do you think David's music helped Saul to feel better?

● Do you have a favorite song?

● How do you feel when you hear it?

Pray: Dear God, thank you for giving us music to praise you and to help express our feelings. Amen.

Encourage the children to enjoy their yummy harps.

A Morsel More

✋ Help children form a rhythm band. Bring to class or make simple instruments for the children to play. Make a cardboard tube kazoo by attaching a square of wax paper to one end of a cardboard tube and securing it with a rubber band. Make a shaker by putting beans, gravel, or rice in a plastic bottle and taping the lid shut or by sealing beans, gravel, or rice between two paper plates. Use two unsharpened pencils to make rhythm sticks. Cut a hole in a shoe box lid, and wrap rubber bands around the box to create a "harp."

✋ Bring in recordings of different kinds of instrumental music. Play the music while the children use crayons to color pictures to represent the way the music makes them feel happy, peaceful, sad, excited.

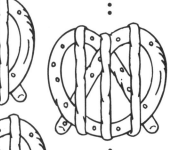

Spice Up the Recipe!

● Use Fruit by the Foot for harp strings. Cut the strings into long strips, and wrap them around the pretzel.

● If baking is an option, bake canned bread sticks that have been bent into harp shapes. Cut ham slices into one-quarter-inch strips, and "glue" them to the harp edges with canned cheese.

David's Hero Sandwiches
God will give us courage.

David's Hero Sandwiches

Terrific Tools:

plastic knives

paper plates (1 per child)

Fun Foods:

hoagie rolls (1/2 roll per child)

mayonnaise

mustard

sliced turkey (1 slice per child)

sliced ham (1 slice per child)

sliced American cheese (1 slice per child)

Before class, slice the rolls in half crosswise. Then split each half lengthwise so that each roll makes two sandwiches.

Spread one side of the roll with mayonnaise and the other with mustard. Place the slices of meat and cheese on the hero sandwich. Top with the second piece of bread.

(From Group Publishing, Inc.'s *Incredible Edible Bible Story Fun for Preschoolers;*
copyright © 1999 Jane C. Jarrell and Deborah L. Saathoff.)

The Bible Story
David Fights Goliath (1 Samuel 17)

Ask:

● What is a hero?

Say: The Israelites needed a hero. The Philistines had come to fight the Israelites. The two armies camped across a field from each other. The Philistines had a giant soldier who was bigger than anyone the Israelites had ever seen. Each day he stood in the field and tried to scare the Israelites. He shouted, "Send out your best warrior to fight me! If he wins, you win. If he loses, you lose." The Israelites needed a hero to protect them from the Philistines. But no one wanted to fight the giant, Goliath. He was too big and too mean and too scary!

One day David came to bring food to his older brothers who were in the Israelite army. He heard Goliath challenge the army. He was amazed that no one would fight. David wasn't very big, but he was filled with the right stuff! Give each child half a hoagie roll on a plate.

Say: **David's heart was pure.** Show the kids how to spread mayonnaise on their bread.

David was strong. Let the children who want mustard spread it on the bread.

David knew God would help him. His God was bigger and stronger than Goliath. Let the kids add the other ingredients to their sandwiches.

David went out to fight the giant. He didn't have a sword. He didn't have a shield. He didn't have armor. He just had the same slingshot he'd always had. He put a rock in it and spun it around and around and around and around, and when it was going fast enough, he let it fly toward Goliath's great big head. Goliath fell down flat. Let the children put the second piece of bread on their sandwiches. **And it was over! David was a hero! These sandwiches are called Hero

Sandwiches. They're little, but they're filled with the stuff that makes them great, just as the stuff God put inside David was what made him great. Ask:

- Why was David a hero?
- Who is your hero? Why?

Pray: Dear God, please fill us with the same good things you filled David with, like courage and trust in you. Thank you for giving us heroes like David to learn from. Amen.

A Morsel More

☞ Take children outside (or find a big, open space inside), and show them how to take giant steps. Ask: How far can you step? How can you measure your giant steps?

☞ Lead children in singing your favorite song about David. Be sure to include the motions.

Spice Up the Recipe!

- Try several different meats and cheeses. Add pickles, cooked bacon, and any other sandwich topping your kids like.

- Using a loaf of wheat bread, hollow out the inside to represent the brook where David found his five stones. Fill the hollowed loaf of bread with five of your favorite sandwich fixings.

David and Jonathan's Friendship Bracelets
We can thank God for friends.

David and Jonathan's Friendship Bracelets

Terrific Tools:

napkins (1 per child)

Fun Foods:

1 box small, circle-shaped cereal   1 package cherry licorice strings

Take a long string of cherry licorice. Thread the cereal onto the licorice until it is the size of a bracelet.

Tie the licorice around someone's wrist.

(From Group Publishing, Inc.'s *Incredible Edible Bible Story Fun for Preschoolers*;
copyright © 1999 Jane C. Jarrell and Deborah L. Saathoff.)

The Bible Story
David and Jonathan (1 Samuel 18)

Ask:
- What is a friend?
- What do friends do?

Say: **David had a special friend. His name was Jonathan. They loved each other very much. Sometimes friends wear special bracelets that are gifts from each other. We call these friendship bracelets.** Give each child a handful of cereal on a napkin and a licorice string.

Jonathan gave David some of his clothes to wear. Ask the children to thread three pieces of cereal onto the licorice string.

He also gave David his bow so he could shoot arrows. Have children string three more pieces of cereal. **He gave David a belt to wear** (have children string more cereal) **and a sword to use in battles.** Have children string more cereal.

Jonathan and David were best friends. King Saul was Jonathan's father. Saul was angry because people were beginning to like David more then they liked him. Saul told Jonathan that Jonathan would never get to be king if David was around. So Saul tried to kill David.

David ran away from Saul. Jonathan told David that he would have to leave so the king could not find him. Have children add more cereal. **David and Jonathan were very sad. David told Jonathan he would miss him.** Have children string remaining cereal. **Jonathan told David that they would be friends for the rest of their lives, even if they couldn't do things together.** Tie each child's friendship bracelet around his or her wrist. Ask:
- Why did Jonathan help David?
- The Bible says, "A friend loves at all times" (Proverbs 17:17a). How do friends help each other?
- What can you do to be a good friend?

Pray: **Dear God, thank you for giving us friends to have fun with and to help. Help each one of us to be a good friend today. Amen.**

Encourage children to enjoy the cereal from their bracelets and to then eat the string!

A Morsel More

✋ Take pictures (instant-print pictures would be great) of each child in the class. Trace each child's hands on a piece of construction paper, cut out the outlines, and write the child's name on them. Glue the hands so that they're joined together in a circle. Then place each child's picture next to his or her hands on a large piece of paper for a bulletin board or hallway wall. Title the display "Our circle of friends."

✋ Give each child an eight-inch square of white paper. Have each child use bright markers or crayons to draw a picture of something he or she likes to do with a friend. Surround the squares with construction paper borders; then put the squares together on a wall to form a "friendship quilt."

✋ Go outside for three-legged races.

Spice Up the Recipe!

● Use alphabet cereal to spell out your children's names.

● Using icing as "glue," stick cereal letters to the top of a cookie or cupcake.

Elijah's Black Birds
We can thank God for providing for us.

Elijah's Black Birds

Terrific Tools:

plastic knives

1 small, round cookie cutter

1 crescent-shaped cookie cutter

wax paper (1 piece for each child)

Fun Foods:

brownies (1 per child)

slivered almonds

small, round cinnamon candies

Before class, cut a brownie for each child. Make sure each brownie is large enough to allow two crescent shapes and one circle to be cut from it.

Cut a circle from the center of a brownie. Place it on a piece of wax paper. Cut two crescents from the remaining brownie. Place one crescent on either side of the circle to resemble bird wings. Stick cinnamon candies on the circle to represent a bird's eyes and a slivered almond to represent its beak.

(From Group Publishing, Inc.'s *Incredible Edible Bible Story Fun for Preschoolers;*
copyright © 1999 Jane C. Jarrell and Deborah L. Saathoff.)

The Bible Story
Elijah Is Fed by Ravens (1 Kings 17)

Ask:
- Who fixes dinner for you when you're hungry?
- What do you do when you're thirsty?

Say: Today we're going to hear about a man named Elijah who had his dinners and drinks delivered to him in a very unusual way.

Elijah was God's prophet. That means that he was a person God had chosen to be his messenger, to tell people the message God wanted to send to them. Let's cut out a circle to remind us of the message Elijah was carrying. Have each child cut a circle from a brownie and place it on a sheet of wax paper.

God chose Elijah to remind the leaders of Israel to worship only God.

Help the children cut one crescent from each brownie. Ask children to place it next to the circle with one point touching the circle. This will resemble a bird's wing, but don't describe it that way to the children.

King Ahab didn't listen to Elijah. He didn't do what God wanted. So God told Elijah to give King Ahab a message. "Because you refuse to obey God," Elijah told King Ahab, "no rain will fall for a long time." And it didn't. Have each child cut a second crescent from a brownie and place it on the opposite side of the circle to resemble the second wing.

Because no rain fell, no plants grew. Because no plants grew, the people had no food. Soon even Elijah had no food. The days were hot ,like this candy. Give each child one cinnamon candy to put on the circle. **The nights were hot.** Give them a second cinnamon candy to put on the circle.

But God took care of Elijah. He showed Elijah a special place where a very small river still ran with water. Elijah lived by that brook and drank its water.

God sent big black birds called ravens to Elijah every morning and every evening. The birds brought bread and meat to Elijah, carrying it in their beaks. Maybe they looked a lot like the birds you have just made. Give each child an almond to place on the circle below the cinnamon candies to represent the bird's beak. Elijah had food to eat and water to drink because God used the birds to take care of him. Ask:

● How does God take care of you?

● How could God use you to help care for others?

Pray: Dear God, thank you for taking care of our needs. Help us to see what we can do to care for others. Amen.

Say: Eat your Black Bird, and remember that while God can use birds to provide for us, he usually uses people. We need to look for ways God can use us to help others.

A Morsel More

🖐 God used birds to provide Elijah's food, but your students can provide food for birds by making bird feeders. Children can tie a piece of yarn around the top of a pine cone, slather the pine cone with peanut butter, and roll it in birdseed for a quick and simple feeder. Or give each child a milk carton of any size, and cut windows from all four sides. Have children color or paint the cartons. Poke two holes through the top of each carton, and tie string through the holes. Give children a supply of birdseed to place in the bottom of each carton.

🖐 Ask the children to bring canned goods for a local charity or food bank.

🖐 Use pictures from magazines and newspapers to make a classroom collage of all the things God provides for us. Include pictures of clothes, homes, toys, food, and family.

Spice Up the Recipe!

● Use refrigerated sugar-cookie dough to make the bird shapes. Bake the "bird" cookies according to package directions, and decorate them with colored sugar, sprinkles, and silver candy balls for eyes.

Elijah's Meal Muffins
God wants us to share with others.

Elijah's Meal Muffins

Terrific Tools:

1 mixing bowl

1 spoon

1 rolling pin

miniature muffin cup liners

measuring cups

Fun Foods:

1 package graham crackers, crushed

1/4 cup melted or liquid margarine

1/4 cup sugar

Before class, crush the graham crackers with a rolling pin, and mix in the sugar.

Put the graham cracker mixture in a bowl. Add the margarine. Put a spoonful of the mixture in each muffin cup liner, and press it down hard. Remove the paper from the muffins before eating.

Note: Variations in humidity will make a difference in how moist the crumb mixture will be. Be ready to add more liquid margarine if the mixture doesn't readily hold its shape when you press it together.

(From Group Publishing, Inc.'s *Incredible Edible Bible Story Fun for Preschoolers;*
copyright © 1999 Jane C. Jarrell and Deborah L. Saathoff.)

The Bible Story
Elijah and the Widow's Jar (1 Kings 17)

Ask:

● What does it mean to share?

● How can sharing make things better?

Say: We can learn something important about sharing from the story of Elijah and the widow who shared with him. Elijah had been living by a creek. God brought him to the creek to give him water to drink. God sent birds to give Elijah food to eat. But one day the creek dried up because there had been no rain. There wasn't any more water for Elijah to drink.

God told Elijah to go to a city called Zarephath. He told Elijah that a woman there would give him food to eat. Elijah did what God told him to do. When he got to the city, he saw a woman picking up sticks to make a fire. He asked her for a drink and a piece of bread.

"I don't have any bread," the woman answered. "I only have a little bit of oil (show kids the liquefied margarine) **and a little bit of flour.** Ask a child to add the graham cracker mixture to the margarine. I am going to bake bread for my son and myself. It will be our last meal because we have no more food." Ask:

● Do you think we can make muffins out of these two simple things? Why or why not?

At first, the widow was afraid that there wouldn't be enough food if she gave some away. Elijah told the woman not to be afraid. Ask a child to stir the mixture. He told her to make the bread as she had planned. Ask another child to stir. **Elijah** asked her to make a little of the bread for him to eat (ask another child to stir) **and then make some for herself and her son.** Ask another child to stir.

Elijah told her that God would make sure that her jars of flour and oil would never be empty until it rained again.

The woman went home and did what Elijah asked her to do. She shared the first bread with Elijah; then she made more for her son and herself. Day after day, she did the same thing, and each day they had enough. God blessed both Elijah and the woman's family through her willingness to share.

Take turns spooning the mixture into the cups. Show children how to press the mixture down hard in each muffin cup. Give the cups an extra squeeze before children unwrap them.

Ask:
- How did sharing help Elijah?
- How did sharing help the woman and her son?

Pray: Dear God, you have given us so many wonderful things. Help us to share them in love with the people around us, and to watch you use them. Amen.

A Morsel More

 Create jars of cornmeal art by layering cornmeal with salt. You can dye the salt by shaking it with several drops of food coloring. Give each child a small clear jar with a screw-on lid. (Baby food jars are ideal.) Layer the different colors in the jars to create designs. You can further illustrate the concept of sharing by giving each child the entire supply of a single color. Help children see that they can create much prettier designs if they share their supplies.

 As a way to share your blessings, sponsor a child from another country through a mission program.

 Give each child a piece of paper and one crayon or marker. Make sure each child has a different color of crayon or marker. Tell the children they must draw a colorful rainbow. Encourage them to figure out that they must share their colors in order to create the pictures.

Spice Up the Recipe!
- Press the graham cracker mixture down far enough to top it with a teaspoon of cherry pie filling, pudding, melted chocolate, or whipped topping.

Naaman's Dip
God will help us to do what we need to do.

Naaman's Dip

Terrific Tools:

measuring cups	1 bowl
1 large spoon or whisk	small cups (1 per child)
spoons	

Fun Foods:

1 package buttermilk ranch seasoning packet	1 cup buttermilk
green food coloring	1/2 cup sour cream
1/2 cup mayonnaise	1 package prepared carrot sticks (1 carrot per child)

Mix the first five ingredients together in a bowl. Spoon into serving cups.

(From Group Publishing, Inc.'s Incredible Edible Bible Story Fun for Preschoolers;
copyright © 1999 Jane C. Jarrell and Deborah L. Saathoff.)

The Bible Story
Naaman Is Healed of Leprosy (2 Kings 5)

Ask:

● **Have you ever had to do something you didn't really want to do? What was it?**

Say: God's helper Elisha told a sick man named Naaman (NAY- uh-mun) to do something Naaman really didn't want to do. Elisha told him to wash himself in the Jordan River and God would make him well. Ask a child to pour the contents of the seasoning packet into the bowl.

Naaman looked at the Jordan River, and he said, "I know there are better rivers than that! I don't want to wash there!" Ask:

● **Why do you think Naaman didn't want to wash in the Jordan River?**

Say: **Maybe he didn't like the way the river smelled.** Let the children smell the buttermilk and then pour it into the bowl. Add a couple of drops of green food coloring.

Say: **Maybe he didn't like the way the river looked.** Let the children look at the bowl with the green mixture. Add the sour cream and mayonnaise, and stir.

Say: Naaman said, "I want Elisha to come wave his hand over me. These spots won't just wash off!" His servants said, "If Elisha had asked you to do something hard, you would have done it. Just follow his directions!"

Naaman had to wash in a special way. Let's each get some of this "river water" so you can do what Naaman did. Give each child some dip and a carrot stick. Say: Pretend that your carrot stick is Naaman.

Naaman did as Elisha had told him. He walked into the Jordan River and washed one time. Ask the children to dip their carrot sticks into the dip and take a bite. Naaman got out, walked back into the Jordan River, and washed again. Dip and eat. Naaman washed **a third time** (dip and eat), **a fourth time** (dip and eat), **a**

fifth time (dip and eat), **a sixth time** (dip and eat), **and a seventh time.** Dip and finish the carrot.

When Naaman came out of the Jordan River after washing the seventh time, his sickness was completely gone! Naaman had done what Elisha had told him to do, and God had healed him. Ask:

● How did Naaman feel about doing what he was asked to do?
● What job is hard for you to do?

Pray: **Dear God, sometimes we have to do things we don't especially like doing. Help us to remember that good things happen when we obey you. Amen.**

A Morsel More

👋 Show children how to work together to clean up an area inside or outside the church. Celebrate completion of the project with a party.

👋 Encourage children as they work a challenging jigsaw puzzle together. A picture puzzle of about twenty-five pieces provides a challenge for three- and four-year-olds. Cover the finished puzzle with puzzle adhesive. Talk about the fact that, by doing something hard, children have been rewarded with a lasting decoration for their classroom.

Spice Up the Recipe!

● Add ham bits, chopped fresh spinach, shredded Parmesan cheese, or water chestnuts to the dip mixture.

● Hollow out a large, round loaf of bread, and pour the dip into the bowl. Cut the bread removed from the loaf into croutons for dipping.

Josiah's Fruit Scrolls
We make God happy when we obey him.

Josiah's Fruit Scrolls

Terrific Tools:

paper plates (1 per child)

wax paper (1 piece per child)

Fun Foods:

dried fruit rolls (1 per child)

bananas (1 per child)

string licorice, 1 piece per child

Unroll a fruit roll. Roll a banana inside the fruit roll. Tie the "scroll" with the string of licorice.

(From Group Publishing, Inc.'s *Incredible Edible Bible Story Fun for Preschoolers*;
copyright © 1999 Jane C. Jarrell and Deborah L. Saathoff.)

The Bible Story
Josiah the Boy King (2 Kings 22)

Ask:

● Do you think children can do important things for God? Why?

Say: Josiah was a boy who became king of Judah when he was only eight years old! He did something very important for God.

The Bible says Josiah was a good king. He got rid of the statues the bad kings before him had made and worshipped. He reminded his people they were to worship only God. Josiah sent workers to fix up the Temple of God. He sent priests to clean the Temple and prepare it for worship.

One day a priest found something very important in the Temple. It was the Israelite's Bible, God's rules for them. The words were written on a scroll. Scrolls were rolled up much as these fruit rolls are rolled. Let's each unroll one of them. Give each child a fruit roll to open and unroll and a paper plate.

No one had read these words for many years. The priest took the scroll to King Josiah. As he read the words, he realized his people's hearts had become tough and empty, just like these fruit rolls. He wanted his people to know about God's rules. Let's fill our fruit rolls up to remind us of Josiah's people being filled with God's rules. Give each child a banana to peel; then show the children how to roll the peeled bananas in the fruit rolls, to resemble stuffed scrolls.

Say: God's Word became a special gift to Josiah's people. It helped his people live in a way that made God happy. Let's add a pretty ribbon to our scrolls to remind us of the gift of God's Word. Help each child tie a string of licorice around his or her scroll.

God was very happy with King Josiah. King Josiah had done what was right. He had obeyed God. And God blessed him. Ask:

● Why is it important to follow God's rules?

● How did Josiah make God happy?

● What can you do to make God happy?

Pray: Dear God, thank you that we don't have to wait until we're grown up to

do things that make you happy. Help us to obey you just as Josiah did. Amen.
Enjoy your scrolls!

A Morsel More

✋ Make mezuzas. Mezuza means "doorpost" and refers to Deuteronomy 6:9 and 11:20, in
which the Israelites were told to write the words of God on the door
frames of their homes. The Israelites made small brass casings that fit on
their door frames. The casings held tiny parchments. The verses from
Deuteronomy 6:4-9 and 11:13-21 were written on the parchment and kept in
the mezuzas. When family members went into or out of the door, they
touched or kissed the mezuza and remembered God's instructions.
Give each child a cardboard tube from a roll of toilet paper. Have the children use scissors to cut small straight slits all around one end of the tube.
Fold the ends in, and use masking tape to secure them, closing one end of
the tube. Help children decorate the tubes with paint, markers, and construction paper or stickers.

✋ Give each child a small piece of paper with the verses from Deuteronomy 6:4-9 copied
on them. Have children roll up the papers and slip them into their mezuzas. Have the children take the mezusas home, and encourage them to tape them to their bedroom doors.
Place one on the door frame of your classroom.

Spice Up the Recipe!

● Use a tortilla for your scroll. Spread a thin layer of cream cheese or butter on the
tortilla, and top it with a slice of smoked turkey or ham. You can use pickle spears on
either end. Roll the tortilla tightly, and tie with a string of cheese.

Jonah's Jumble
We can thank God for his forgiveness.

Jonah's Jumble

Terrific Tools:

1 mixing bowl	1 large spoon
fabric netting	ribbon

Fun Foods:

1 package thin pretzel sticks	1 bag fish-shaped crackers
1 can honey-roasted peanuts	

Before class, cut the netting into 6-inch squares.

Pour all ingredients into the mixing bowl. Stir to combine. Spoon the Jonah's Jumble into the net squares.

Lift up the sides of the netting, and tie it with ribbon.

(From Group Publishing, Inc.'s *Incredible Edible Bible Story Fun for Preschoolers;*
copyright © 1999 Jane C. Jarrell and Deborah L. Saathoff.)

The Bible Story
Jonah and the Whale (Jonah 1–2)

Ask:

● When have you not wanted to do something you were asked to do?

Say: Jonah was asked to do something he didn't want to do. God asked him to go to Nineveh and tell the people there that God did not like the bad things they were doing. God was planning to destroy their city. If God did that, their city would be nothing more than a jumble of sticks where their homes once were. Ask a child to pour the pretzel sticks into the bowl.

Jonah didn't want to obey God. Instead of going to Nineveh, he got on a boat that was going away from Nineveh! God knew exactly where Jonah was. He sent a big storm. The sailors on the boat wondered why they were in a storm. Jonah knew. He told them it was because he had tried to run away from God. He told the sailors to throw him off the ship and the storm would stop. So the sailors threw Jonah into the sea, among all the little fish. Ask a child to pour the fish-shaped crackers into the bowl.

And as Jonah swam among those little fish, a big fish came along and swallowed him up! Remove the mixing bowl from the table. Jonah spent three days inside that fish. He prayed a lot. He asked God to save him. Then God made the fish spit Jonah out onto dry land. Bring the mixing bowl back.

God said, "Now, go to Nineveh." This time Jonah did what God told him to do. He told the people of Nineveh that God would destroy their city because of the bad things they were doing. The people of Nineveh listened to Jonah. They were very sorry they had done the bad things that had made God unhappy. They prayed. They asked God to forgive them, just as Jonah had prayed from inside the big fish. So God gave the people of Nineveh a second chance, just as he had given Jonah a second chance. God did not destroy their city. Instead he gave them the sweet gift of forgiveness. Add the honey-roasted nuts.

Give children each a square of netting. Help them place spoonfuls of the mixture in the center of their netting. Be ready to help them close the netting with ribbon. Say: **Jonah's story helps us to remember that God is forgiving. Let's tie our fish nets with a ribbon to remind us of God's gift of forgiveness.**

● **When does God forgive us?**

Pray: **Dear God, sometimes we do things that make you unhappy, but because of Jesus, you forgive us when we ask you to. Thank you for being forgiving. Amen.**

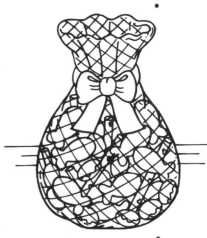

A Morsel More

🖐 Use brown eye shadow on kids' hands or arms to show how disobedience to God leaves us unclean. Use a baby wipe or makeup remover to show how God's forgiveness cleans us when we tell God we're sorry for doing wrong.

Spice Up the Recipe!

● Add fish-shaped pretzels, Skittles candies, miniature marshmallows, vanilla chips, butterscotch chips, dried bananas, and raisins to the mix.

New Testament

Angel Announcement Cakes
God wants us to share his good news.

Angel Announcement Cakes

Terrific Tools:

paper plates (1 per child)

plastic forks (1 per child)

1 serrated knife (adult)

1 spoon

Fun Foods:

1 purchased angel food cake

1 jar chocolate sauce

1 eight-ounce container of whipped topping

maraschino cherries with stems (1 per child)

Before class, use the serrated knife to cut the angel food cake into 2-inch slices.

Spoon 2 tablespoons of chocolate sauce over each piece of cake. Top with whipped topping and a cherry.

(From Group Publishing, Inc.'s *Incredible Edible Bible Story Fun for Preschoolers*; copyright © 1999 Jane C. Jarrell and Deborah L. Saathoff.)

The Bible Story
Angels Announce the Birth of Jesus (Luke 1)

Ask:

● What is the best news you've ever had?

● How did you get your good news?

Say: The good news we're going to learn about today was delivered by an angel! One day an angel was sent by God to give a wonderful message to a young lady named Mary. Let's put some angel food cake on our plates to remind us of the angel. Give each child a two-inch slice of angel food cake on a paper plate.

"Greetings!" the angel said to Mary. "God has chosen you for something very special." Does this chocolate sauce look special to you? Let's add it to remind us of the angel's message. Let each child spoon two tablespoons of chocolate sauce over his or her cake.

Mary was frightened. She had never seen an angel before.

"Don't be frightened," the angel said. "God loves you. You are going to have a baby. You are to name him Jesus. He will be the Son of God." Wow! That was even more special! Let each child add a spoonful of whipped topping to the cake slices.

"How can this be?" Mary asked the angel.

"Nothing is impossible with God," the angel answered.

"I believe you," Mary said. "I will do whatever God wants." And that was the sweet end of their conversation. Let each child place a cherry on top of the whipped topping.

● How do you think Mary felt about the angel's news?

● Jesus is good news for *everyone*. Who can you tell this good news?

Pray: Dear God, thank you for sending an angel with good news for Mary. Help us to share your good news with the people we know. Amen.

A Morsel More

 Play Good News Hot Potato, using a beanbag, stuffed toy, or other small, soft object. Have the children sit or stand in a circle. Play music while the children pass the "potato" around the circle. Stop the music without warning. The person holding the potato must share some good news with the group.

 Make angels. Give the children angel shapes cut from lightweight cardboard (such as shirt boards). Let the children decorate their angels using yarn and fabric scraps, and glitter or pieces of ribbon and trim. Provide gold pipe cleaners to make halos for the angels. Glue the angels onto craft sticks to make puppets. Or glue them to cardboard cones covered with cotton balls (to look like clouds) to make tree toppers.

 Sing "Joy to the World" or "Hark! the Herald Angels Sing."

Spice Up the Recipe!

● Make a layered dessert out of the angel food cake and your favorite toppings. Tear the angel food cake into large, bite-sized pieces. Line a large bowl with the cake pieces. Pour the chocolate sauce over the cake, and top it with strawberries, whipped topping, and chopped nuts. Add another layer of the angel food cake, and layer strawberries, whipped topping, nuts, and cherries. Top with extra whipped topping and a cherry with a stem.

Manger Haystacks
We can thank God for the gift of Jesus.

Manger Haystacks

Terrific Tools:

1 medium bowl

paper plates (1 per child)

1 tablespoon

measuring cups

1 large spoon

Fun Foods:

2 large cans chow mein noodles

1/2 cup marshmallow cream

1/2 cup peanut butter

1/2 cup miniature chocolate morsels

Place all the ingredients into a bowl, and stir thoroughly to combine. Spoon 2 tablespoons of the noodle mixture onto a paper plate, and form the mixture into a "manger."

(From Group Publishing, Inc.'s *Incredible Edible Bible Story Fun for Preschoolers*;
copyright © 1999 Jane C. Jarrell and Deborah L. Saathoff.)

The Bible Story
Jesus' Birth in the Manger (Luke 2)

Ask:

● What is the best present you've ever received?

● Why is it the best?

Say: **Just before Jesus was born, Mary and Joseph had to go to a city called Bethlehem. Many people had to go to Bethlehem. So many people came into the city that there were no places for the visitors to stay. All the beds were full, and people were sleeping on the floors. Joseph and Mary finally found a place to sleep in a stable that was full of hay for the animals who lived there.** Ask a child to dump the chow mein noodles into the bowl.

That night, Mary's baby was born. Mary and Joseph wanted the baby to have a soft place to lie. Ask a child to add the marshmallow cream to the bowl and another to add the peanut butter.

Mary and Joseph named the new baby Jesus because an angel had told them Jesus was the perfect name for God's Son. Ask a child to add the chocolate morsels to the bowl.

Mary wrapped Jesus in special baby clothes. Have children take turns stirring the mixture until the ingredients are thoroughly combined.

She made a bed for Jesus in a manger, a box that held the food for the animals to eat. Jesus, God's most precious gift to the world, slept in a box filled with hay that might have looked like the mixture we just made. Spoon two tablespoons of the noodle mixture onto each child's paper plate, and ask the children to form the mixture into a place for the baby to sleep. Ask:

● What gift did God give the world?

● Why is God's gift so very special?

Pray: Dear God, thank you so much for the precious gift of Jesus. You didn't give us something that would get old or broken or lost. You gave us your Son. Thank you. Amen.

A Morsel More

🖐 Help children make thank you notes to God. Have the children decorate folded paper. Use stamps, or write the words "thank you" on the front of the notes for the children. Ask them to draw pictures and sign their names inside the cards.

🖐 Let the children wrap blocks or empty boxes with precut squares of wrapping paper.

Spice Up the Recipe!

● Try lots of different stir-ins: honey-roasted peanuts, coconut, white chocolate chips, raisins, dried apricots, and even M&M's.

Stars on High
We can give gifts to Jesus.

Stars on High

Terrific Tools:

1 star-shaped cookie cutter

paper plates (1 per child)

plastic knives

Fun Foods:

wheat bread (2 pieces per child)

apple butter

peanut butter

Use the cookie cutters to cut star shapes out of 2 pieces of wheat bread. Spread 1 star shape with peanut butter. Spread the other star shape with apple butter. Put the 2 stars together to make a star sandwich.

(From Group Publishing, Inc.'s *Incredible Edible Bible Story Fun for Preschoolers;* copyright © 1999 Jane C. Jarrell and Deborah L. Saathoff.)

The Bible Story
Wise Men Follow the Star (Matthew 2)

Ask:

● What do we do for a new baby or for someone on his or her birthday?

Say: When Jesus was born, God put a special star in the sky. Have each child cut out one star from the wheat bread and set it aside.

Some wise men living in a country to the east saw the special star. They knew it meant a baby king had been born. Have the children each cut out a second star. They decided to go see this new king. They chose special presents to give the new baby.

The wise men couldn't call someone and ask directions to where the new king could be found. They didn't have newspapers or television to tell them where the baby had been born. So the wise men followed the star. They had to travel a long way. Have each child spread a star with peanut butter.

The wise men followed the star until they found the place where Jesus was staying. Have each child spread apple butter on a second star.

They bowed down before Jesus and gave him presents. They gave him gold, precious oils, and perfumes called frankincense and myrrh. Have children each put their two stars together to form a star sandwich. Ask:

● Why do you think the wise men gave Jesus presents?

● What presents can we give Jesus?

Pray: Dear Jesus, just like the wise men we want to give gifts to you, too. Help us to remember to love and obey as our gifts to you. Amen.

A Morsel More

👋 Have a birthday party for Jesus. Decorate the room for a birthday party with banners, streamers, balloons, and table coverings. Let the children make party hats. Sing "Happy Birthday to You" to Jesus. Have children draw pictures as gifts for Jesus, wrap the pictures in packages, and place them on the table.

👋 Collect toys for needy children in your church or town. Explain that Jesus tells us that when we do something for someone in his name, it's as though we have done it for him. So if they give toys to children who would otherwise do without and give them in Jesus' name, it's giving a gift to Jesus.

Spice Up the Recipe!

Try making a box cake in a jellyroll pan (a cookie sheet with sides). After the cake has baked and cooled, cut star shapes from the cake, and place them on wax paper. Frost with purchased frosting, and sprinkle with candies. For a healthful selection, try spreading the cake with a pure fruit spread and sprinkling it with golden raisins.

Wedding Wonder Water
God's changes are good.

Wedding Wonder Water

Terrific Tools:

1 large pitcher

1 long-handled spoon

small cups (1 per child)

Fun Foods:

4 cups water

1 can frozen grape juice concentrate, thawed

6 ice cubes

Place the ice cubes in the pitcher. Pour the water into the pitcher. Add the thawed grape juice concentrate. Stir thoroughly and pour into cups.

(From Group Publishing, Inc.'s *Incredible Edible Bible Story Fun for Preschoolers;* copyright © 1999 Jane C. Jarrell and Deborah L. Saathoff.)

The Bible Story
Jesus Turns Water Into Wine (John 2)

Ask:

- What happens when something changes?
- When are changes bad?
- When are changes good?

Say: One day Jesus and his friends went to a wedding. The wedding included a special party with food to eat and wine to drink. The people danced and sang. It was a wonderful and fun time for everyone who was there. Ask a child to place the ice cubes in the pitcher and stir. Listen to the happy sound of these ice cubes as they touch each other! They almost sound like guests at a party.

During the party, Jesus' mother came to him and told him something was wrong. Make sure the ice cubes are still. The party was getting very quiet. There was no more wine for the guests to drink.

Jesus told the workers to get six large stone jars that were sitting close by. He told the workers to fill the jars with water. The workers did what Jesus told them to do. Ask a child to pour the water into the pitcher. That was the first change, and it was good, but Jesus didn't stop with that!

Then Jesus told them to dip some water out of a jar and take it to the people. The servants dipped the water out of the jar, but it wasn't water anymore! It was wine! That was the second change, and it was *really* good. Ask a child to pour the thawed grape juice concentrate into the pitcher.

The servants kept dipping wine from the water jars and serving it to the people. Have the children take turns stirring the mixture until it is thoroughly combined. The people drank it.

One man said it was not only *good*, it was the *best* wine that had been served throughout the whole party. The guests didn't know where the wine had come from but the workers knew. They knew it had been water but Jesus had turned it into wine. It was a miracle-change from God, and God's changes are good! Pour the mixture into cups, and encourage children to enjoy the drink. Ask:

● **How did Jesus honor his mother?**

● **How can you honor your parents?**

Pray: Dear Jesus, while you were here on earth, you showed us the way God wants us to live. Help us to learn to honor our parents just as you honored your mother. Amen.

A Morsel More

👋 Have the children draw pictures that show how they will honor their parents during the coming week.

👋 Help children make gifts to give to their parents. For example, children could make hand prints on paper; then you could print "Helping Hands" underneath the prints, along with the children's ideas for helping their parents.

Spice Up the Recipe!

● Pour prepared grape juice into ice-cube trays, and freeze. Stir the frozen grape-juice cubes into the grape juice.

Storm Shakers
God will help us when we are afraid.

Storm Shakers

Terrific Tools:

1 large container with lid

1 ladle

small cups (1 per child)

Fun Foods:

4 cups water

2 cups sugar

2 packages blue soft-drink mix

1 small bag crushed ice

Pour the water into the container. Add the sugar, the soft-drink mix, and the crushed ice. Place the lid securely on the container, and shake. Ladle the Storm Shakers into small cups.

(From Group Publishing, Inc.'s *Incredible Edible Bible Story Fun for Preschoolers;*
copyright © 1999 Jane C. Jarrell and Deborah L. Saathoff.)

The Bible Story
Jesus Calms the Storm (Mark 4)

Ask:

● What things make you feel afraid?
● What do you do when you feel afraid?

Say: **Jesus has always been great at helping people who are afraid. One day Jesus taught a great crowd of people beside a lake until very late in the day.** Ask a child to pour the water into the container with the lid. Ask another child to pour in the drink mix. **This blue drink kind of reminds me of the lake Jesus taught beside. Jesus got very tired and asked his friends to go with him to the other side of the lake. They got into a boat and began to sail to the other side.** Ask a child to add the sugar to the container.

Suddenly it began to get colder, and the wind began to blow. Ask a child to add the crushed ice to the container. Place the lid securely on the container. **The winds blew stronger.** Ask a child to shake the container. **The waves crashed higher.** Shake. **They crashed so high that water began to come into their boat.** Shake. **The boat was tossed up and down.** Shake. **The boat was about to sink.** Shake. **Jesus' friends were very frightened.** Shake for the last time. Set the container on a flat surface.

All this time Jesus had been sleeping on a pillow in the back of the boat. His friends woke him up. "How can you sleep?" they asked. "Don't you care that we're all about to drown?"

Jesus got up and told the wind to stop blowing. And it did. He told the waves to be still. And the water became completely calm. Everything was quiet and peaceful. Take the lid off the container.

"Why were you so afraid?" Jesus asked. "Don't you know I will take care of you?" Jesus' friends were amazed. "Even the wind and water obey Jesus," they said. Ladle the Storm Shakers into small cups, and enjoy! Ask:

- Why were Jesus' friends afraid?
- What did Jesus' friends do?
- What can you do when you feel afraid?

Pray: Dear Jesus, thank you that we can tell you the things that make us frightened and you will help us. Amen.

A Morsel More

✋ Have each child draw a picture of something that makes him or her feel afraid. (A dark room, animals, clowns, scary TV shows or movies, bugs, and visits to the doctor are all common preschool fears.) Display a picture of Jesus, and ask the children to give their fears to Jesus by putting their drawings in front of Jesus' picture. Pray: Dear Jesus, we give you these fears and ask that you help us to be calm and peaceful on the inside just as you made the waters calm and peaceful. Amen.

✋ Help children create their own wind-tossed boats using corks, clay, paper, toothpicks, and straws. Show children how to put a little clay or modeling dough on one end of a cork to weight it down. Poke a toothpick into the opposite end of each cork. Slide a small square of paper over the toothpick to form the sail. Adjust the clay and sail until the "boats" float in a large washtub or water table. Encourage children to propel the boats through the water by blowing through the straws.

Spice Up the Recipe!

- Make fruit shakers by adding your favorite puréed fruits such as strawberries, raspberries, or blueberries.

Sweet Seeds
We can let God's love grow in our hearts.

Sweet Seeds

Terrific Tools:

1 small bowl	measuring cups
small cups (1 per child)	straws cut in half (1/2 straw per child)
small edible flowers such as pansies or violets (1 per child)	small spoons (1 per child)

Fun Foods:

1 cup chocolate sandwich cookies, crushed	1/4 cup coconut, dyed green
1 six-ounce box instant chocolate pudding, prepared according to package directions, or canned pudding	
1/2 cup shelled sunflower seeds	

Place 2 tablespoons of crushed cookies into each cup. Spoon chocolate pudding over the crushed cookies. Top with the prepared green coconut. Sprinkle the sunflower seeds over the coconut. Insert the straw into the cookie-pudding mixture, and add the flower by inserting the stem into the straw.

(From Group Publishing, Inc.'s *Incredible Edible Bible Story Fun for Preschoolers;*
copyright © 1999 Jane C. Jarrell and Deborah L. Saathoff.)

The Bible Story
Jesus and the Parable of the Sower (Luke 8)

Ask:

● What must seeds have before they can grow into plants?

Say: **One day Jesus told this story about seeds growing into plants. A farmer went to plant seeds in his field. He scattered the seeds all over the ground.** Toss some sunflower seeds onto a table.

Some of his seeds fell on a path. Birds came and ate those seeds. Pick up the seeds.

Some seeds fell in dirt that was full of rocks. Toss some more seeds on the table. **The seeds grew, but the plants dried up because there were too many rocks.** Pick up the seeds.

Some seeds fell on ground that was covered in weeds. Toss some seeds out. **The seeds grew, but the weeds crowded out the plant.** Pick up the seeds again.

Some seeds fell into good dirt. Have each child spoon two tablespoons of crushed cookies into his or her small cup. **They fell deep into the ground where no birds could get them. The roots could grow deep in the soil that had no rocks. The plants could grow tall because no weeds blocked the sun.** Sprinkle a few sunflower seeds over the cookie crumbs. **The farmer cared for the soil and kept it moist.** Have the children spoon pudding over the crushed cookies in the cups.

The people asked Jesus what his story meant. He told them the seeds were the news about God's love. Have the children sprinkle green coconut over the pudding in the cups.

The ground is people's hearts. Some people hear about God and his love for them, but their hearts are closed. They don't understand, and they don't love God or try to obey him. They are like the seeds that fell on the path or in the rocks and weeds.

Other people hear about God and his love for them, and they understand. Have each child insert a straw into his or her cup. **God's love grows in their hearts like the strong plants that grew in good soil.** Have each child place a flower in his or her straw. Ask:

● What can we do so that God's love will grow in our hearts?

Pray: Dear God, thank you for giving us your love. Help us to love and obey you so that your love will grow strong in our hearts. Amen.

A Morsel More

☞ Plant seeds in small paper or plastic foam cups. Marigold seeds or bean seeds sprout quickly and produce hardy plants.

☞ Bring in several large, flat rocks. Have the children paint or decorate them as reminders not to let God's Word get choked out by rocky soil.

Spice Up the Recipe!

● Make a Merry Seed Meadow snack in a 13x9-inch pan. Put two cups of the cookie crumbs in the bottom of the pan. Top with pudding from two six-ounce packages of instant pudding; sprinkle with coconut, chopped nuts to represent gravel, miniature marshmallows, chopped cherries, and seeds. Place whole cherries and whole strawberries on toothpicks to form flowers, and place them randomly over the layers. Add more of your favorite things to make the snack look like a meadow complete with seeds and flowers.

Miracle Corn
God uses little things.

Miracle Corn

Terrific Tools:

1 electric popcorn popper

1 large paper bag

small paper bags (1 for each child plus 1 for the popcorn kernels)

Fun Foods:

1 cup popping corn

oil (if required)

2 cups fish-shaped crackers

Place the popping corn into a small brown bag. Prepare the popcorn popper to pop the corn. (NOTE: Follow the specific directions that came with your popcorn popper.) Pop the popcorn, and see how one cup of corn grows. Place the popped corn in a large brown bag. Fill small brown bags with popped corn and crackers to represent the loaves and fishes.

The Bible Story
Jesus Feeds the Five Thousand (John 6)

Prepare the popcorn popper, using all necessary safety precautions, including taping down the cord if necessary. Ask:

● **Do you think good things come in big packages or little packages? Why?**

Say: Today we're going to hear about a big crowd and a little package. One day more than five thousand people came to listen to what Jesus was teaching. The people listened all morning. They listened all afternoon. At dinner time, they were still listening to Jesus. Jesus' friends asked Jesus to tell the people to go home so they could get something to eat. But Jesus said, "No, we'll feed them."

"We don't have enough money to buy food for this many people!" one of his friends said. Another one of his friends said, "Here is a boy with a little bag of food, but it's not enough to share with five thousand people!" Hold up the paper bag containing the corn, and shake the bag. Put the popcorn kernels in the popper. While the kernels are popping, say: Jesus told the people to sit down. He took the boy's meal and thanked God. The food from that little boy's lunch kept on coming and coming and coming, like this popcorn! But the little boy didn't have popcorn, he had bread and fish. Jesus did a miracle!

Jesus gave the people as much food to eat as they wanted. Have each child put a handful of popcorn and some fish-shaped crackers in a small brown bag.

There was so much food that Jesus' friends picked up twelve baskets of leftovers after the people had eaten from the five loaves of bread and the two fish.

The people who were there knew that fish doesn't puff up like popcorn. Neither does bread. They knew that this wonderful miracle and Jesus himself must be sent from God. Enjoy your miracle meals! Ask:

● **How did Jesus use the little boy's lunch?**

● What little thing do you have that you could share with others?

Pray: **Dear Jesus, thank you for showing us that you can use little things. Help us remember to give you whatever we have so that you can use it. Amen.**

A Morsel More

👏 Use the leftover popcorn to make a collage.

👏 Make paper-doll chains. Fold a sheet of paper crosswise, accordion-style, into four sections. Draw the shape of a figure on the top fold of paper, making sure the drawing includes the folds on both edges in at least one place. Use scissors to cut the figure out, being careful not to cut the folded edges in several places on the figure. Open the paper to reveal a row of figures. Have children decorate the figures by drawing clothing, hair, and facial features on each one. Show children that what looks like one doll expands into many, just as the boy's lunch expanded to feed many people.

Spice Up the Recipe!

● Popcorn makes a great base for trail mix. Just add raisins, carob chips, dried bananas, and animal crackers. Toss the ingredients together, and store the mixture in an airtight container. Add other favorites to make your trail mix even better.

Marshmallow Sheep
God looks for anyone who's lost.

Marshmallow Sheep

Terrific Tools:

wax paper (1 piece per child)

small plastic spoons (1 per child)

small paper plates (1 per child)

small plastic knives (1 per child)

Fun Foods:

1 package large marshmallows

1 jar marshmallow cream

1 package pretzel sticks

1 package miniature marshmallows

raisins (2 per child)

Set out 2 large marshmallows and 2 small marshmallows. Using the marshmallow cream, "glue" the 2 large marshmallows together to form the body of the sheep. Use the marshmallow cream to glue the small marshmallow onto the top of one end of the large marshmallows to form a head. Glue the other small marshmallow onto the other end of the sheep to form the tail. Stick two raisins onto the small marshmallow head to form the sheep's eyes. Stick 4 pretzels into the sheep for the legs.

(From Group Publishing, Inc.'s *Incredible Edible Bible Story Fun for Preschoolers*; copyright © 1999 Jane C. Jarrell and Deborah L. Saathoff.)

The Bible Story
Jesus the Good Shepherd (Luke 15)

Ask:

● What do you do when you lose something important?

Say: To teach people about God, Jesus told a story about a shepherd who lost something important. In Jesus' story, the shepherd had a hundred sheep. He watched over them carefully. He made sure they had sweet grass to eat and cool water to drink. He knew every one of those sheep and loved them all. Let's make little sheep to remind us of the shepherd's flock. Give each child two large marshmallows, two small marshmallows, four pretzel sticks, and two raisins on a paper plate. Show the children how to construct the sheep, and help them "glue" the marshmallows together.

The shepherd counted the sheep every day. Let's count our sheep. Count all the sheep. We have [number] sheep, but every day the shepherd counted a hundred sheep. One day he counted only ninety-nine. Oh, no! He counted again to be sure. He was missing one! He didn't just shrug his shoulders and say, "Oh, well. I still have ninety-nine sheep." Instead, he looked and looked and looked until he found the one lost sheep. When he found it, he put it on his shoulders and carried it home. He called all his friends and neighbors together and said, "Be happy with me! I have found my lost sheep!"

Jesus told the people that God is like the shepherd. He loves all of his people. He knows each of them. When one disobeys him, that person is like a lost sheep. God misses that person the same way the shepherd missed the lost sheep. When that person is sorry for disobeying and comes back to God, it makes God happy. God celebrates like the shepherd who found his lost sheep. Ask:

- How does God look for us?
- Why does God look for us?

Pray: Dear God, thank you for looking for us when we disobey you. Thank you for being a good shepherd for us, your sheep. Amen.

Let the children eat their marshmallow sheep.

A Morsel More

🖐 Tie dish towels or pieces of fabric and headbands or string around children's heads as shepherds' headdresses. Hide a single toy sheep somewhere in the classroom, and have the children search for it as if they were shepherds. Have a celebration when the sheep is found.

🖐 Play Hide-and-Seek.

Spice Up the Recipe!

- Give the little sheep chocolate chip eyes and a scarf made from Fruit by the Foot.
- Make woolly sheep by covering them with thin layers of marshmallow cream and sprinkling them with coconut.
- Make black sheep by dipping the marshmallows in chocolate before assembling the sheep.

King's Crowns

We can celebrate because Jesus is our King.

King's Crowns

Terrific Tools:

paper plates (1 per child)

Fun Foods:

cupcakes (purchased or baked ahead of time)   1 can frosting

1 large package gumdrops or jelly beans

Before class, frost the cupcakes.

Decorate the top of each cupcake with gumdrops or jelly beans to resemble a crown.

(From Group Publishing, Inc.'s *Incredible Edible Bible Story Fun for Preschoolers;*
copyright © 1999 Jane C. Jarrell and Deborah L. Saathoff.)

The Bible Story
Jesus Enters Jerusalem (Luke 19)

Ask:

● What kinds of occasions do we celebrate?

Say: Jesus and his disciples were getting ready to celebrate the Jewish holiday called Passover. Two of Jesus' friends went to get a donkey. Jesus had told them where to find it. Jesus told them to tell the owner that the Lord needed it.

Jesus' friends put their coats on the donkey's back. Then Jesus got on the donkey and rode toward the city of Jerusalem. Give each child a frosted cupcake on a paper plate.

Some people put their coats on the ground in front of the donkey Jesus was riding. Have the children each add a "jewel" to their cupcakes.

They waved branches they had cut from palm trees. Then they laid them on the road in front of Jesus' donkey. Have children each add another jewel.

They began to praise God with joy. They shouted, "Hosanna!" and "Blessed is the king who comes in the name of the Lord!" Have children each add two more jewels.

The people followed Jesus into Jerusalem. They praised God for all the wonderful things they had seen Jesus do. Have children each add another jewel.

The people were celebrating Jesus as king. See the crown you've made during their celebration? Ask:

● What can we do to celebrate Jesus as king?

Pray: Dear God, thank you for sending Jesus as our king. We want to say, "Hosanna," and "Bless the king who comes in the name of the Lord." Amen.

A Morsel More

✋ Make or use existing rhythm instruments to form a band. Have the children play the instruments and sing "Ho-ho-ho-hosanna," or other praise songs.

✋ Have children join a parade. Have them use rhythm instruments and wave palm branches. (You can either supply real palm branches or help kids make them from construction paper.)

✋ Use prefabricated border for bulletin boards to form a crown for each child. Let children decorate the border with stickers, construction paper and glue, or markers. With each "jewel" they add, have children give a reason to celebrate Jesus as king.

Spice Up the Recipe!

● Add miniature M&Ms, Skittles, or any other small, colorful candies.

● Add dried fruits and nuts for a healthful touch to your King's Crowns.

Broken Bread
God wants us to remember what Jesus did for us.

Broken Bread

Terrific Tools:

paper plates (1 per child)

measuring spoons

plastic knives

small cups (1 per child)

Fun Foods:

flour tortillas (1 per child)

honey or strawberry preserves (1 teaspoon per child)

butter (1 teaspoon per child)

grape juice

Tear a tortilla into pieces. Mix the butter with honey or strawberry preserves. Spread the butter mixture onto each piece of the tortilla.

Serve the snack with grape juice.

The Bible Story
Jesus and the Last Supper (Mark 14)

Ask:

● What helps you remember important things?

Say: Jesus wanted his disciples to remember him, so he gave them a special way to do it. One night Jesus and his friends were eating a special meal together. Jesus gave his disciples a piece of flat bread. Give each child a tortilla.

Jesus knew it would be the last meal he would eat with his friends before he died. Jesus thanked God, broke the bread into pieces, and shared it with his friends. Ask the children to tear the tortilla into pieces. Give each child a teaspoon of butter and a teaspoon of honey or strawberry preserves. Ask the children to mix the honey or preserves with the butter. Let them spread the butter mixture onto each piece of the torn tortilla.

Fill the small cups with grape juice. Say: Next Jesus took a cup and thanked God again and gave it to his friends. All of them drank from it. Let the children eat their snacks and drink the juice. Say: Jesus told his friends, "Whenever you eat in this special way, remember me." Ask:

● What do we do to remember Jesus?

Pray: Dear Jesus, help us to always remember the things you taught us and all you have done to show us how much you love us. Help us to show you our love in return. Amen.

A Morsel More

✍ Show children how to play Memory (or Concentration) using pictures of church items, such as a Bible, a cross, a church with a steeple, a picture of Jesus, a cup and a loaf of bread, a stained-glass window, and a child in prayer. Make sure every picture has an identical match. Glue the pictures on index cards. Turn the cards face down, and have the children take turns turning the pictures over two at a time.

✍ Play a memory game by showing the children a tray of about seven to ten everyday items, such as a toothbrush, Bible, pencil, fork, glass, quarter, rubber band, ball, and block. Let the children look at the items for one or two minutes. Put the tray away, and ask the children to name as many items as they can remember. Before revealing the tray again, remove two or three items; then ask children to identify the missing items.

Spice Up the Recipe!

● Spread a layer of cream cheese and strawberry preserves on each tortilla. Roll up the tortilla; then drizzle chocolate over it. Slice the rolled tortillas, and top the slices with whipped cream.

Resurrection Butterflies
God can give us new life.

Resurrection Butterflies

Terrific Tools:

1 teardrop-shaped cookie cutter (Squeeze a circle together at one point to form a teardrop.)

wax paper

plastic knives

paper plates (1 per child)

small bowls for colored sugars

Fun Foods:

poundcakes, sliced into ½-inch slices. (1 cake per 3 kids)

licorice sticks (1 per child)

whipped topping

colored sugars or cake decorations

Place 4 slices of poundcake on a plate. Using the cookie cutter, cut a teardrop shape out of each slice. Place a licorice stick lengthwise in the center of a plate. Put 2 teardrops on each side of the licorice stick to form butterfly wings. Spread whipped topping over each of the cake pieces. Sprinkle the colored sugars over each of the teardrops to color the butterfly wings.

(From Group Publishing, Inc.'s *Incredible Edible Bible Story Fun for Preschoolers;* copyright © 1999 Jane C. Jarrell and Deborah L. Saathoff.)

The Bible Story
Jesus' Resurrection (Luke 24)

Ask:

● **What happens to a caterpillar?**

Say: **Jesus died and was placed in a tomb. But the tomb became kind of like a butterfly's cocoon.** Give each child a paper plate with a licorice stick placed lengthwise on it to represent the butterfly's body. Give each child four half-inch-thick slices of poundcake on a piece of wax paper.

We don't know exactly what happened inside the tomb. But we know that God was working. Let each child cut one teardrop from one piece of poundcake and place it next to the licorice stick to make one butterfly wing.

Very early on Sunday morning, some women took special spices to Jesus' grave to finish the preparations for burying him. They were sad, and they worried about how they would move the big stone that had been placed in front of the cave. Let each child cut a second teardrop from a slice of cake and place it on the plate next to the licorice stick for the second butterfly wing.

When the women got to the tomb, the stone was already rolled away. When they went inside, Jesus' body was gone. The women didn't understand what had happened. Let each child cut a teardrop from a third piece of cake and place it on the plate for the third wing.

Two angels wearing clothes as bright as lightning suddenly stood in front of the women. The women were very afraid. They bowed their heads. Let each child cut the final teardrop from the last piece of cake and place it on the plate to complete the butterfly.

The angels said to them, "Why would you look for someone alive in a tomb? Jesus isn't here, he is alive!" Have each child spread the completed butterfly with whipped topping.

The women stepped back from the tomb. They weren't sad and worried anymore. They told their wonderful news to Jesus' friends. Let children each sprinkle some colored sugar on the butterflies.

At first, Jesus' friends didn't believe the women when they told them Jesus was alive. But the women were right! Jesus did come back to see them. He really was *alive!* Add any remaining colored sugar to the butterflies. Ask:

● How was Jesus' time in the tomb like the butterfly's time in a cocoon?

Pray: Dear God, thank you for making Jesus alive after he was dead. You are so powerful and good. Thank you for butterflies that remind us of new life. Amen.

A Morsel More

✍ Give each child a row of six egg cups cut lengthwise from the bottom half of an egg carton. Show children how to add pipe cleaner antennae to one end of carton and how to draw eyes. Then cut construction paper butterfly wings to an appropriate size for the caterpillars. Provide bits of tissue paper, crayons, or markers to decorate the wings. Show kids how to glue the wings onto the caterpillar backs to change the caterpillars into butterflies.

✍ Plant seeds in clear plastic cups. (Place the seeds close to the outside edge.) Talk about how the seeds look before they're planted. Point out how the seed changes as the plant grows. Tell children that the plant could not exist if the seed did not change in the ground.

Spice Up the Recipe!

● Spread each teardrop or wing shape with frosting, and sprinkle each piece with colored sprinkles.

 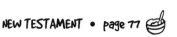

Miracle Fish Sandwiches
God wants us to serve others.

Miracle Fish Sandwiches

Terrific Tools:

1 fish-shaped cookie cutter

paper plates (1 per child)

wax paper

1 rolling pin

resealable plastic bags

Fun Foods:

white bread (1 to 2 slices per child)

ham, thinly sliced (1 slice per child)

American cheese, sliced (1 slice per child)

Before class, remove the crusts from each piece of white bread, and roll the slices out flat on a piece of wax paper.

Using the cookie cutter, cut fish shapes from two slices of rolled bread, a slice of cheese, and a slice of ham. Stack the bread, cheese, and ham to form a "fish" sandwich.

Place the scraps in the plastic bag for snacks later.

(From Group Publishing, Inc.'s *Incredible Edible Bible Story Fun for Preschoolers;*
copyright © 1999 Jane C. Jarrell and Deborah L. Saathoff.)

The Bible Story
Jesus and the Disciples' Breakfast (John 21)

Ask:

● What does it mean to serve someone?

● When does someone serve you?

● When do you serve others?

Say: **After Jesus rose from the tomb, he visited his friends.** Give each child a piece of rolled bread.

One evening Peter and some friends were fishing with nets far from the shore. Jesus watched from the shore as the men threw their nets out and brought them up empty, again and again, all night long. They didn't know Jesus was watching them from the shore.

Early in the morning, Jesus called out, "Did you catch any fish?"

"No," they answered.

"Throw your nets on the other side of the boat," he said.

So Jesus' friends threw the nets on the other side of the boat. All at once fish filled the net. Maybe there were orange fish. Give children each a piece of cheese, and let them cut fish shapes. **Maybe there were pink fish.** Give children each a slice of ham, and let them cut out fish shapes. **Maybe there were white fish.** Let the children cut out the bread. **There were so many fish they couldn't pull the net into the boat!**

That's when Peter realized it was Jesus on the shore! He was so excited he jumped out of the boat and swam to the shore.

Jesus made a campfire on the beach and cooked fish and bread for them to

eat. **"Come and have breakfast,"** he said to his friends. Have the children place the cheese and the meat on the bread.

Let each child serve his or her fish sandwich to a friend. Ask:

● **How did Jesus serve his disciples?**

● **What can you do to serve someone else this week?**

Pray: **Dear God, please help us to serve others around us. Thank you for showing us how to do that by serving your disciples. Amen.**

A Morsel More

✍ Let the children go fishing with fishing poles made from sticks or dowels. Tie a string on one end of the stick. Attach a small magnet to the loose end of the string. Cut out (and laminate if possible) construction paper fish. Attach a paper clip to each fish. Use a net to scoop up the children's catch as they pick up the fish.

✍ Make newspaper boats to float in the water. Fold a sheet of newspaper in half by bringing the top half down at the center fold. Then fold the top two corners down toward the bottom center, but leave about two inches of the bottom edge below the point where the top corners meet. Fold the bottom edges up on each side. Bring the outside corners together, and flatten sideways into a square. Holding the open points toward you, fold the loose corners up to meet on each side, forming a triangle, and bring the outside corners together again and flatten sideways into a square. Gently pull the top two loose corners open to form a boat. Let children float the boats in a sink or washtub. Encourage children to see how many paper clip "fish" the boats can hold.

✍ After children have prepared the snacks, help them serve them to another class or other guests.

Spice Up the Recipe!

● Add a thin layer of herbed cream cheese to each fish-shaped piece of bread. Next add thinly sliced ham or roast beef to make a fish "submarine" snack.

Pentecost Pinwheels
We can thank God for the gift of his Holy Spirit.

Pentecost Pinwheels

Terrific Tools:

paper plates (1 per child)

1 cutting board

1 measuring spoon

1 knife

1 small spoon

Fun Foods:

8 ounces softened cream cheese

large apples (1 per child), cored and cut into fourths (Prepare ahead, and dip into Fruit Fresh or lemon juice.)

maraschino cherry halves (1 per child)

1 jar caramel sauce

Place 1 tablespoon of cream cheese in the center of a plate. Use a small spoon to make a well in the center of the cream cheese. Fill in the cream cheese well with caramel sauce. Place 4 apple quarters evenly around the cream cheese and caramel. Place a maraschino cherry half in the middle of the caramel to form the center of the pinwheel.

The Bible Story
The Holy Spirit Comes at Pentecost (Acts 2)

Ask:

● **What does the wind look like?**

● **How do you know it's real?** Help the children understand the difference between the wind and things that are blown by the wind. Explain that we never see wind, only the things moved by it.

Say: **After Jesus rose from the tomb, he stayed and taught his friends for forty days. Then Jesus went to heaven to be with God the Father. Before Jesus left, he told his friends to stay in Jerusalem. Jesus said to wait and God would send someone very important to them.** Give each child a paper plate.

So Jesus' friends waited together in Jerusalem just as he had told them. A special holiday called Pentecost was celebrated while they were there. Many people came from far and near to celebrate Pentecost in Jerusalem. Jesus' friends celebrated too. Let each child place one tablespoon of cream cheese in the center of the plate. Then use a small spoon to make a well in the center of the cream cheese, and pour in the caramel sauce.

While they were together, they suddenly heard a sound like a strong wind blowing through the room. Ask:

● **What are some toys that are fun to play with in the wind?**

We're going make these snacks look like pinwheels. Pinwheels remind us of the wind Jesus' friends heard.

Jesus' friends were filled with God's Holy Spirit. This was what Jesus had told

them to wait for. Let each child place one apple quarter so that it touches the cream cheese well. **Now that Jesus was in heaven, God's Spirit would still be with his friends here, helping them and teaching them, much as Jesus had done.** Let the children place the rest of the apple quarters around the cream cheese and caramel.

"This is what God promised," Jesus' friend Peter told the people. Let each child place a maraschino cherry in the middle of the caramel to form the center of the pinwheel. Ask:

● **We can't see God. How do we know God is real and with us?**

Pray: **Dear God, thank you for the gift of your Holy Spirit. Thank you for sending the Holy Spirit to live with us and to help us know you are real. Amen.**

A Morsel More

✋ Make or fly kites. Or help children make nonflying kites. Cut a piece of construction or butcher paper into a large diamond. Decorate the kite shape with markers, paint, or stickers. Glue or staple string from tip to tip. Add a length of string to the center where the first two strings intersect. Staple or glue a crepe paper streamer to the bottom to form the tail.

✋ Let the children make windsocks by decorating sheets of paper. Show children how to roll the paper lengthwise into a cylinder and fasten it in place using tape or staples. Using tape, staples, or glue, attach crepe paper streamers to one end of the cylinder. Attach a string or yarn hanger to the opposite end.

Spice Up the Recipe!

● Use different fruits to make the pins on the pinwheel. Try bananas, pears or even angel food cake. Use anything that you think will taste good dipped in the caramel and cream cheese.

● Add chopped honey-roasted peanuts and coconut to the dip.

Gingerbread Families
We can thank God for the family of believers.

Gingerbread Families

Terrific Tools:
paper plates

plastic knNes

Fun Foods:
2 packages gingerbread men cookies

sprinkles

2 or 3 colors canned frosting

small red cinnamon candies

Place 2 or 3 gingerbread people on a plate. Using frostings, sprinkles, and candies, decorate the gingerbread people to represent family members or church members.

(From Group Publishing, Inc.'s *Incredible Edible Bible Story Fun for Preschoolers*;
copyright © 1999 Jane C. Jarrell and Deborah L. Saathoff.)

The Bible Story
The Early Church Shares (Acts 2)

Ask:

● What is a family?

● What do members of a family do for each other?

Say: **After Pentecost many people joined Jesus' friends as believers. They believed Jesus was the Son of God too. These new believers listened carefully to all that Jesus' friends taught them about Jesus.** Give each child a paper plate with two or three gingerbread people on it.

All the believers shared their lives. They ate their meals together. They prayed together. They shared their belongings with each other. They helped each other when they needed it. They met together every day. Ask one or two children to set out the different frostings with the plastic knives.

The believers were happy and honest and faithful to God. They praised God. Ask a child to set out the sprinkles.

More and more people decided to believe in Jesus because they saw the way the believers treated each other. Ask a child to set out the cinnamon candies. Let the children decorate their gingerbread people to represent themselves and one or two family members. Before they eat their creations, set out all the decorated cookies so children can see the "church family" that they have created.

Ask:

● How were the first believers like a family?

● How are believers today like a family?

● How can we share with other members of the family of believers?

Pray: Dear God, thank you for our families who love and care for us. Please show us how we can love and care for our church family, too. Amen.

A Morsel More

✋ Make mission banks for the children to take home and fill with coins to donate to a church-sponsored mission. An empty clear-plastic soda or bottled water bottle makes a good bank. Decorate the bank by turning it into a tree, a monkey, or a piggy bank by adding construction paper cutouts and pipe cleaners for features. Cut a slit in the bottle for the coins. Donate the money collected to a church-sponsored charity. (Use small plastic bottles to make individual banks for the children, or make one large bank to display in class.)

✋ "Adopt" a child through an international mission program as a long-term project; or adopt a needy family through a local program, and provide assistance throughout a holiday season.

✋ Have the children draw pictures of their families. Post the pictures on the wall with the title "Our Church Family."

Spice Up the Recipe!

● If a microwave is handy, try melting some milk-chocolate morsels with a little milk for forty seconds on medium heat. Stir, and microwave again on medium for another forty seconds until chocolate is melted. Dip one side of the gingerbread people into the melted chocolate and then into a bowl full of sprinkles. You can also use melted vanilla morsels, and make one side vanilla and one side chocolate.

Mighty Chariots
We can tell others about Jesus.

Mighty Chariots

Terrific Tools:

plastic kniNes

paper plates or squares of wax paper (1 per child)

Fun Foods:

string cheese (1/2 stick per child)

pretzel sticks

cheddar cheese, cut into 2-inch cubes

Cut the cheese into "wheels." Poke a pretzel stick into the center of each wheel. Poke the free end of each pretzel into a cube of cheddar cheese. Place 2 pretzel wheels each on the right and left sides of the cheese chunk to form the chariot.

(From Group Publishing, Inc.'s *Incredible Edible Bible Story Fun for Preschoolers;* copyright © 1999 Jane C. Jarrell and Deborah L. Saathoff.)

The Bible Story
Philip and the Ethiopian (Acts 8)

Say: **Philip served God in the church at Jerusalem. As he traveled, he met many people. One day as he traveled down a desert road, he met an important man who worked for the queen of a neighboring country. This man was returning to his country after worshipping in Jerusalem, and he was reading the Bible as his chariot moved along the road.** Ask:

● **What do you think the chariot might have looked like?**
● **Why do you think the man was reading the Bible?**

Say: **Let's make some chariots before I finish telling you the story.** Give each child a paper plate or a square of wax paper, a plastic knife and one-half stick of string cheese. Say: **Let's make some wheels for our chariots. Slice your cheese stick into circles.** Give the children time to complete this task. Then say: **Count out four circles of cheese and lay them on one side of your plate. One...two...three...four! You can eat all the cheese circles you cut except those four.** Show the children how to poke a pretzel into the center of each cheese circle to form a wheel. Then pass out the cheddar cheese cubes.

Say: **We'll use a chunk of cheese to form the wagon part of the chariot where people would sit.** Show the kids how to insert each wheel into the cheese chunk to resemble a chariot.

Say: **The man in the chariot invited Philip to come inside his wagon and explain the words he was reading in the Bible. Philip used the words the man was reading to help him understand the good news about Jesus. The man was so excited that he become a Christian right then and there! The man went home happy, and Philip went on to tell others about Jesus.**

A Morsel More

✋ Let the kids create a path for the tiny chariots to move across by laying four-inch pieces of celery stalks end to end.

✋ Sing this song to the tune of "The Farmer in the Dell":

The Bible brings good news!

The Bible brings good news!

Tell the people everywhere

The Bible brings good news!

Spice Up the Recipe!

● Let the kids crumble crackers or pretzels to form a "desert" to serve the chariots on.

● Use a quarter-teaspoon measuring spoon to hollow out each chariot. Set a gummy bear inside to represent Philip.

Heavenly Hospitality Treats
We should show kindness to others.

Heavenly Hospitality Treats

Terrific Tools:

paper plates (1 per child)

napkins

1 serving tray

small plastic knives

small cups (1 per child)

Fun Foods:

1 package round butter crackers

1 small box raisins

1/2 cup ham chunks

1/2 cup strawberries, sliced

1 bunch grapes

1 small jar peanut butter

1 jar processed cheese spread

3 ounces softened cream cheese

1 container of juice

Using butter crackers as the base for all of your Heavenly Hospitality Treats, decorate the first batch by spreading peanut butter over the crackers and topping them with raisins. Spread some cheese over the second batch of crackers, and top with chunks of ham. Spread a thin layer of cream cheese over the third batch of crackers, and top with strawberry slices.

Place all of the treats on a large round tray. Place a bunch of grapes in the center, and serve guests the Heavenly Hospitality Treats along with juice to drink.

(From Group Publishing, Inc.'s *Incredible Edible Bible Story Fun for Preschoolers*;
copyright © 1999 Jane C. Jarrell and Deborah L. Saathoff.)

The Bible Story
Lydia's Hospitality (Acts 16)

Ask:

● What do you do when guests visit your home? Why?

Say: The Bible gives us many examples of how wonderfully people treated their guests. One of these stories is about Lydia, whose guests were missionaries who traveled to many different countries to tell people about Jesus and his love for them.

When Paul, a missionary, and his friends came to Lydia's town, they found Lydia and some other women praying at the river. Paul and his friends began to tell them about Jesus.

Lydia believed Jesus was the Son of God. Lydia and her family were baptized. She knew Paul and his friends were guests in their city. She knew they did not have anywhere to stay. She knew they would need food to eat. So Lydia invited Paul and his friends to stay at her house. Maybe she made special treats like the ones we're going to make. Let the children prepare the crackers as described in the recipe.

Paul and his friends stayed with Lydia and her family while they taught people in that city about Jesus and his love for them. Ask one of the students to place the bunch of washed grapes in the center of the tray. Have the children help place all of the treats around the grapes. Invite guests to share your hospitality tray. Ask:

● **How does preparing something special show kindness?**

Pray: **Dear God, please help us to be kind to our friends. Please show us ways to be helpful to our family and friends today. Amen.**

A Morsel More

👋 Have children practice manners. Show the children how to make polite introductions and have them practice with each other. Talk about proper table manners while enjoying a snack around a table. Discuss the ways manners can help us show kindness to others.

Spice Up the Recipe!

● Use small party breads instead of crackers. Select different flavors and colors of bread. Stick a toothpick in each slice of bread, and place a small piece of fruit on top of each toothpick.

Tasty Tents
God wants us to work hard for him in whatever we do.

Tasty Tents

Terrific Tools:

brightly colored paper plates (1 per child)

Fun Foods:

1 box graham crackers

1 large tube chocolate icing

1 small bag thin pretzel sticks

Squirt a generous line of chocolate icing down one long side of a graham cracker. Lean the second cracker against the first cracker at the line of icing to form a tent. Place pretzel sticks at either end of the graham cracker tent to serve as the poles to hold the tent up.

(From Group Publishing, Inc.'s *Incredible Edible Bible Story Fun for Preschoolers;*
copyright © 1999 Jane C. Jarrell and Deborah L. Saathoff.)

The Bible Story
Paul the Tentmaker (Acts 18)

Ask:

● What jobs do you do at home now?

● What jobs do your parents do at home? What jobs do they do away from home?

Say: **Paul believed in Jesus. He believed Jesus is God's Son and that people should love and obey him. He went from city to city telling people all about Jesus. He told them that they could have God's love in their lives and that they could live forever with God in heaven.** Give each child two unbroken graham crackers and two pretzel sticks.

But teaching people wasn't the only thing Paul did. Paul made tents. It was his job. One day he met two other tentmakers, a husband named Aquila and his wife, whose name was Priscilla. They became believers in Jesus too. Let each child squirt a thick line of chocolate icing along the long side of one graham cracker.

Paul worked with them, and together they made tents to sell to other people. Paul, Aquila, and Priscilla made tents all week. Have the children prop the two graham crackers together to form a tent with the chocolate icing acting as "glue" to hold the two sections together. **On the days the Jewish people gathered to worship God, Paul would tell them about Jesus, God's Son. Many people believed in Jesus because of Paul's teaching.** Let each child place pretzel sticks at each open end of the tent to serve as tent poles. Ask:

● Paul's job was making tents. **What jobs do you think you might like to do when you grow up?**

Pray: **Dear God, you have given us all work to do and the ability to do it. Help us to do the work we have to do as if we were doing it just for you. Amen.**

A Morsel More

✋ Invite parents or other adults to give a "Career Day" talk. Ask them to tell the students about the work they do and how their faith in Jesus makes a difference in how they do their work.

✋ Have the children draw self-portraits doing jobs they think they would like to have when they grow up. Make a career collage with the pictures.

✋ Drape a large sheet over a classroom table to make a large tent. Have a story time inside the tent.

Spice Up the Recipe!

● Frost graham crackers with your favorite frosting before assembling the tent. Sprinkle miniature chocolate morsels or miniature M&M's on the sides of the tent.

Colorful Chains

We can sing and praise God, even when bad things happen.

Colorful Chains

Terrific Tools:

plastic knives

1 small bowl

paper plates (1 per child)

water

paper towels

Fun Foods:

different colors and flavors of fruit by the foot cut into 6-inch strips (5 strips per child)

Place 5 fruit strips of different colors on a plate. Make each strip into a circle, and link the circles together to form a chain. Close the circles by dabbing a small amount of water on the ends and pressing them together.

(From Group Publishing, Inc.'s *Incredible Edible Bible Story Fun for Preschoolers;*
copyright © 1999 Jane C. Jarrell and Deborah L. Saathoff.)

The Bible Story

Paul and Silas in Jail (Acts 16)

Ask:

● How do you feel when someone has been unkind to you or treated you unfairly?

● What do you do?

Say: **Some very unfair things happened to Paul the missionary. Paul had a good friend named Silas. Paul and Silas traveled together telling everyone they met about Jesus. Many people listened to their words and believed in Jesus. People who believed in Jesus were called Christians.** Give each child a plate with five different colors of fruit strips on it.

Not everyone believed Paul and Silas. They didn't like Christians and tried to get them to stop telling people about Jesus. In one city people put Paul and Silas in jail. They put chains around Paul's and Silas' feet so they couldn't walk. Have each child make a circle using one of the strips. Let children dab water on the ends and press them together to make the circle.

Paul and Silas didn't worry, even though they were in chains and in jail. They prayed to God. They sang songs to God. The other people in the jail listened to them. They listened to their prayers. They listened to their songs. Have each child link a second circle with the first one and use water to seal the second circle.

In the middle of the night, the ground shook with an earthquake. Everyone was surprised. But then the doors to the jail flew open! The chains on the prisoners fell off! Have each child link a third circle onto the chain.

The man in charge of the jail woke up and ran to see what had happened. He was afraid that all the prisoners had run away. Have each child link a fourth circle onto the chain.

Paul and Silas called to him, "We are all here." The jailer was amazed. He

knew something had happened that only God could do. He asked Paul and Silas what he should do. Have each child link a fifth circle onto the chain.

"Believe in Jesus," they told him. And he did. He let Paul and Silas out of jail. The jailer took them to his home and took care of them. He gave them food to eat. The jailer's family members all became Christians that night. Ask:

● Why do you think Paul and Silas could sing and praise God after so many bad things had happened to them?

● When will you sing and pray to God this week?

Pray: Dear God, thank you for always being with us, no matter what happens. Help us to remember that you are always here, always loving us wherever we are. Amen.

A Morsel More

✋ Make paper chains.

✋ Sing praise songs. Use rhythm instruments to accompany the songs.

✋ Use one-pint plastic berry baskets as jail cells. Make puppets by drawing features on the ends of craft sticks. Decorate the puppets with fabric scraps and yarn. Let the children tell the Bible story using the puppets and basket.

Spice Up the Recipe!

● Purchase a 13x9-inch cake, and frost it using a thin layer of canned frosting. Cut Fruit by the Foot into strips long enough to lay over the top of the cake. Place the fruit strips two-inches apart over the cake's surface to look like prison bars. Decorate the top of the cake with one of the chains.

Bible Boats
God helps us to be brave.

Bible Boats

Terrific Tools:

paper plates (blue, if available—1 per child)

1 cutting board

plastic knives

1 large sharp knife for adult use

Fun Foods:

1 large cantaloupe, cleaned, peeled, and sliced into 10 equal wedges (1 cantaloupe for every 10 children)

1 round watermelon slice, peeled and cut into 10 equal triangle-shaped wedges (1 slice of watermelon for every 10 children)

1 large pineapple, cored, seeded and cut into six 6-inch straight strips (1 pineapple for every 10 children)

maraschino cherry halves without stems (2 per child)

Place a cantaloupe slice at the bottom of each plate to form the hull of the ship. When completed, the ship will lie on its side on the plate. Place a pineapple piece in the center of each cantaloupe to form the sail's mast. Place a watermelon slice next to the pineapple to form a sail. Place a cherry at each end of the cantaloupe wedge.

(From Group Publishing, Inc.'s *Incredible Edible Bible Story Fun for Preschoolers*;
copyright © 1999 Jane C. Jarrell and Deborah L. Saathoff.)

The Bible Story
Paul Is Shipwrecked (Acts 27)

Ask:

● Have you ever been very frightened? What did you do?

Say: Paul was in jail because he told people about Jesus. Many kings and other rulers asked him about his beliefs. Finally, they sent Paul to Caesar, the king who was in charge of all the rulers. Give each child a blue paper plate.

It was a long trip to Rome, where Caesar lived. There were no cars, trains, or airplanes, so Paul went on a boat. Some of Paul's friends went with him on the trip. Give each child a cantaloupe wedge to place at the bottom of the paper plate to form a boat lying on its side, flat against the plate.

When the boat left for Rome, a gentle breeze turned into a terrible storm. It lasted for several days. The first day the sailors pulled the lifeboat onto the ship. They tied ropes under the ship to try to hold it together. They lowered the anchor. Have each child place the strip of pineapple on the plate, touching the cantaloupe hull, to form the mast.

The second day of the storm, the crew began to throw things overboard. For many days they couldn't see the sun or the stars because the storm was so terrible. Many people on the ship gave up hope of living through the storm. Have each child place a watermelon slice next to the pineapple strip to form a sail.

Paul stood up in front of the sailors and told them that he was a child of God. He told them an angel had said that he would live to tell Caesar about

Jesus. He also told them that everyone else on the ship would live through the storm. Paul told the sailors to be brave because he had faith that God would do what he said he would do. Give each child one maraschino cherry to place at one end of the cantaloupe boat.

After fourteen days the ship ran aground on some sand. Everyone got off the ship and either swam or floated on pieces of wood. Soon all the people were safe on a nearby island, just as the angel had said. Give each child a second maraschino cherry to place at the other end of the boat. Ask:

● Why were the sailors frightened? Why wasn't Paul frightened too?

● The next time you feel frightened, what can you do to help you be brave?

Pray: Dear God, thank you that when we know you and know you are always with us, we can be brave too, just as Paul was. Amen.

A Morsel More

👆 Help children make sailboats from milk cartons. You'll need a half-gallon milk carton to make each boat. Cut the carton in half lengthwise. Cut one half in half again horizontally. Use a sharp pencil to poke a hole in the top of the bottom fourth. Put the section with a hole upside down in the lengthwise half of the first milk carton at the squared end. Push a straw into the hole to form the mast. Cut a construction paper rectangle to make the sail, and attach it to the straw. These boats really float, so put them in a sink or washtub for kids to enjoy.

👆 Help the children act out the story of Paul's shipwreck. Appoint one child to play Paul and everyone else to play the ship's passengers and crew. Put the chairs together to form the ship, or mark off an area of the room with masking tape. Let children rock and roll with the waves and pass ropes between them and "around" the ship. Begin to throw cargo "overboard." Prompt Paul to speak his words of hope and encouragement. Run "aground," and let children pretend to swim and float to a designated island.

Spice Up the Recipe!

● Bible Boats are boat-shaped fruit salads, but you can transform them into desserts by piling on your favorite fruits, sprinkling with miniature marshmallows, and adding a dollop of whipped topping.

Group Publishing, Inc.
Attention: Product Development
P.O. Box 481
Loveland, CO 80539
Fax: (970) 679-4370

Evaluation for *Incredible Edible Bible Story Fun for Preschoolers*

Please help Group Publishing, Inc., continue to provide innovative and useful resources for ministry. Please take a moment to fill out this evaluation and mail or fax it to us. Thanks!

● ● ●

1. As a whole, this book has been (circle one)

not very helpful   very helpful

1   2   3   4   5   6   7   8   9   10

2. The best things about this book:

3. Ways this book could be improved:

4. Things I will change because of this book:

5. Other books I'd like to see Group publish in the future:

6. Would you be interested in field-testing future Group products and giving us your feedback? If so, please fill in the information below:

Name _____

Street Address _____

City _____ State _____ Zip _____

Phone Number _____ Date _____

TEACH YOUR PRESCHOOLERS AS JESUS TAUGHT WITH GROUP'S *HANDS-ON BIBLE CURRICULUM*™

Hands-On Bible Curriculum™ **for preschoolers** helps your preschoolers learn the way they learn best—by touching, exploring, and discovering. With active learning, preschoolers love learning about the Bible, and they really remember what they learn.

Because small children learn best through repetition, Preschoolers and Pre-K & K will learn one important point per lesson, and Toddlers & 2s will learn one point each month with **Hands-On Bible Curriculum**. These important lessons will stick with them and comfort them during their daily lives. Your children will learn:

- •God is our friend,
- •who Jesus is, and
- •we can always trust Jesus.

The **Learning Lab**® is packed with age-appropriate learning tools for fun, faith-building lessons. Toddlers & 2s explore big **Interactive StoryBoards**™ with enticing textures that toddlers love to touch—like sandpaper for earth, cotton for clouds, and blue cellophane for water. While they hear the Bible story, children also *touch* the Bible story. And they learn. **Bible Big Books**™ captivate Preschoolers and Pre-K & K while teaching them important Bible lessons. With **Jumbo Bible Puzzles**™ and involving **Learning Mats**™, your children will see, touch, and explore their Bible stories. Each quarter there's a brand-new collection of supplies to keep your lessons fresh and involving.

Fuzzy, age-appropriate hand puppets are also available to add to the learning experience. What better way to teach your class than with the help of an attention-getting teaching assistant? These child-friendly puppets help you teach each lesson with scripts provided in the **Teacher Guide**. Plus, your children will enjoy teaching the puppets what they learn. Cuddles the Lamb, Whiskers the Mouse, and Pockets the Kangaroo turn each lesson into an interactive and entertaining learning experience.

Just order one **Learning Lab** and one **Teacher Guide** for each age level, add a few common classroom supplies, and presto—you have everything you need to inspire and build faith in your children. For more interactive fun, introduce your children to the age-appropriate puppet who will be your teaching assistant and their friend. No student books are required!

Hands-On Bible Curriculum is also available for elementary grades.

Exciting Resources for Your Children's Ministry

No-Miss Lessons for Preteen Kids

Getting the attention of 5th- and 6th-graders can be tough. Meet the challenge with these 22 faith-building, active-learning lessons that deal with self-esteem…relationships…making choices…and other topics. Perfect for Sunday school, meeting groups, lock-ins, and retreats!

ISBN 0-7644-2015-1

The Children's Worker's Encyclopedia of Bible-Teaching Ideas

New ideas—and lots of them!—for captivating children with stories from the Bible. You get over 340 attention-grabbing, active-learning devotions…art and craft projects…creative prayers…service projects… field trips…music suggestions…quiet reflection activities…skits…and more—winning ideas from each and every book of the Bible! Simple, step-by-step directions and handy indexes make it easy to slide an idea into any meeting—on short notice—with little or no preparation!

Old Testament   ISBN 1-55945-622-1
New Testament   ISBN 1-55945-625-6

"Show Me!" Devotions for Leaders to Teach Kids

Susan L. Lingo

Here are all the eye-catching science tricks, stunts, and illusions that kids love learning so they can flabbergast adults…but now there's an even *better* reason to know them! Each amazing trick is an illustration for an "Oh, Wow!" devotion that drives home a memorable Bible truth. Your children will learn how to share these devotions with others, too!

ISBN 0-7644-2022-4

Fun & Easy Games

With these 89 games, your children will *cooperate* instead of compete—so everyone finishes a winner! That means no more hurt feelings…no more children feeling like losers…no more hovering over the finish line to be sure there's no cheating. You get new games to play in gyms…classrooms…outside on the lawn…and as you travel!

ISBN 0-7644-2042-9

Order today from your local Christian bookstore, or write: Group Publishing, P.O. Box 485, Loveland, CO 80539.